# PRAISE FOR
## *TEAM OF DESTINY*

This is a hoops story you will LOVE!
Jerry and Chris capture the sensational
and dramatic championship journey by
Tony Bennett and his tenacious Cavalier team.
UVA was Awesome Baby and so is this book!"

*– Dick Vitale*

# TEAM
## OF
# DESTINY

*INSIDE VIRGINIA BASKETBALL'S RUN TO
THE 2019 NATIONAL CHAMPIONSHIP*

## JERRY RATCLIFFE
## CHRIS GRAHAM

WITH ADDITIONAL REPORTING BY ZACH PERELES, SCOTT RATCLIFFE & SCOTT GERMAN

FOREWORD BY RALPH SAMPSON

**To order additional copies of this book, contact:**
Augusta Free Press
200 S. Wayne Ave. #1193
Waynesboro, VA 22980
(540) 949-6574
www.augustafreepress.com/bookshelf
crystal@augustafreepress.com

# RALPH SAMPSON
# Foreword

On April 13, 2019 as I walked across the field at Scott Stadium on the campus of University of Virginia, my alma mater and now the 2019 NCAA men's basketball national champs, I reflected on the past 40 years since I first arrived on the Grounds at UVA.

It was exactly 40 years to the day that I took my official visit to the campus, also my mother, Sarah Sampson's, birthday, now 81 years old, and my memories flooded me. As I approached the podium to speak to 20,000-plus fans, I could only feel the excitement of the moment, the exhilaration in the crowd … finally, the dream came true.

Last season when the Cavs lost to a No. 16 seed in the first round of the NCAA Men's Basketball Tournament, something that has never been done before in the history of the game, we all wondered how the coaches, players, fans and University would bounce back. The outcome was nothing short of magical. A sensational turnaround for us all.

Some may say that this is the greatest college basketball story in history, while others have challenged the UVA system. However, building a legacy at UVA started many years ago, with players, coaches, fans, teacher and, yes, even the Good Old Song.  Yes, it may have taken 40 years to climb to the top of men's college basketball as national champs, but no one can take away the strength and depth of the relationships we all made over the years.

It is an honor for me to be able to celebrate the greatest college basketball story in history with a true UVA trusted and knowledgeable sportswriter, Jerry Ratcliffe, who has captured all the dramatic moments of the Cavaliers' incredible ride to this historic moment for Wahoo sports.

Jerry and Chris have lived and seen it all, even before my time. I highly recommend this book to every basketball fan across the globe. This story translates to all who know defeat and how to overcome it!

*Ralph Sampson*
*UVA Grad 1983*
*Naismith Hall of Fame 2012*

# CONTENTS

# PART I
## The Championship Run

JON GOLDEN

# CHAPTER 1
# Monday night in April

Everyone had nervous energy to expend. But the Virginia Cavaliers, a year and 23 days past the biggest upset in college basketball, if not sports, history, weren't showing it.

Kyle Guy and Ty Jerome, the faces of the team's exhaustively chronicled 74-54 loss to UMBC in the first round of the 2018 NCAA Tournament, after which Jerome had to answer a question from long-time *Roanoke Times* writer Doug Doughty to the effect that he did, in fact, know that, yes, indeed, that was the first time a No. 1 seed had lost to a No. 16 seed in tournament history, were as loose as the proverbial goose, alternatively playing dodgeball and shooting into imaginary hoops at midcourt during what was supposed to have been a boring chest-pass drill.

Guy and Jerome, a little earlier, had been working with De'Andre Hunter, who had missed that loss to UMBC with a broken wrist sustained in Virginia's ACC Tournament semifinal win over Clemson, on a jump-shooting drill, in which freshman Francisco Caffaro, a highly-touted 7-foot center from Argentina, who was redshirting in 2018-2019, provided what was supposed to be token defense.

Except that, Caffaro, whose reach seems to extend close to nine and a half feet, was doing his job a little too well.

Guy, Jerome and Hunter, Virginia's Big Three, were running off imaginary screens before catching passes from whoever's turn it was, then they were to elevate over Caffaro to get a shot off, basically just over his outstretched hands.

Guy and Jerome seemed to be in rhythm. Loose. Calm. Relaxed.

Hunter couldn't seem to get untracked against Caffaro's closeouts.

A shot, short, hit the front rim. Next time through, he was long. Another bounded awkwardly off the backboard, and Hunter hadn't called bank, or thought it.

No biggie. It was just warmups.

Stay loose, was the mantra for Virginia.

Texas Tech, the Red Raiders, on the other end, looked ready to go to war.

Hunter was Virginia's stud, a certain lottery pick, projected to go as high as fifth in the 2019 NBA Draft, should he choose to declare, as expected.

Texas Tech had its own Hunter, in Jarrett Culver, the 2019 Big 12 Player of the Year.

Culver, warming up, looked locked in. Matt Mooney, the graduate transfer from South Dakota, was even more locked in, after a 22-point night in the national semifinals had helped the Red Raiders past Michigan State.

Brandone Francis, the 6-foot-5 senior guard, a sharpshooter off the bench, was the cucumber on his end, Joe Cool, and he seemed almost too serene, like he was up to something, and it would turn out later, spoiler alert, that he would be.

The tension in U.S. Bank Stadium, which would house more than 72,000 fans all told on that first Monday night in April that everybody in college basketball aspires to be playing on, was too much even for the sharpest and thickest of knives.

It had been a tense day all told for both programs and fan bases in and around Downtown Minneapolis.

The UVA contingent, some 130 or so of them, began the day early, around 7:30 a.m., with a Run With Jim, as it has become known. The new UVA president, Jim Ryan, is an avid runner, and upon arriving on Grounds in 2018, he began making it known that people who wanted to join him on his daily runs were welcome.

The tradition grew, and when UVA Athletics teams were engaged in high-profile games away from Grounds, for example, the football team, on its way to the program's first bowl win in more than a decade, at Charlotte's Belk Bowl, the previous December, people in town for the event would Run With Jim through the streets of wherever.

Ryan seemed taken aback at the turnout for his Run With Jim in Minneapolis, which took the group over and then back again the Mississippi River, snow from a harsh winter still lining the river banks.

CHRIS GRAHAM

Runners mingled in the city park, The Commons, in the shadow of U.S. Bank Stadium, for a good half-hour afterward, not wanting to leave, because, what else were they going to do for the next 12 hours, but fret over something over which they had no control?

The place to be was a few blocks away, at the team hotel, The Marquette, which came to take on almost religious significance for the UVA faithful in the Twin Cities for the Final Four.

SCOTT RATCLIFFE

Shortly after noon local time, still more than eight hours to tip, hundreds of orange- and blue-clad fans gathered in the hotel atrium, for no apparent reason, other than to be around other orange- and blue-clad fans.

A nearby indoor mall was a WahooPalooza, with hundreds more fans in what was effectively an encampment kind of setup.

Former UVA president Teresa Sullivan was among the 'Hoos killing time and nervous energy, chatting with fans, talking about how she'd just ridden an elevator down to the main floor of the mall with Jerome, and how cool and loose and in the moment he seemed to be, and how that was a good sign.

Everybody who was anybody in Wahoo Nation was there, or rumored to be there – Ralph Sampson, Tiki Barber, Joe Harris, Justin Anderson.

It was so densely packed there, honestly, that it was hard to tell exactly what was going on.

Until there was a sighting.

UVA has a lot of celebrity starpower. You've got your sports celebrities, the Sampsons, the Chris Longs, the TV personalities like Katie Couric and Tina Fey.

Jayden Nixon suddenly appeared, carrying a boxed lunch.

You'd have thought, from the reaction of the faithful in the mall, that John Lennon was leading The Beatles across Abbey Road.

A few minutes later, it was Jack Salt, the redshirt senior who seemed to have been on Grounds since Edgar Allan Poe lived on The Lawn.

The seas parted. Camera phones recorded the moment, for posterity.

It wasn't long before Tony Bennett, the pied piper of Wahoo Nation, had his own boxed lunch.

CHRIS GRAHAM

You would think Elvis had just walked out of a 7-Eleven.

For the faithful, it was a new experience, Monday in April, in a sport that Virginia fans claim as the one most near and dear to their hearts.

The Sampson Years, 1979-1983, had whetted their appetites. There was only one Final Four to show for the four years with the three-time national player of the year, but then came the surprise run to a second Final Four the year after Sampson was the No. 1 pick in the 1983 NBA Draft, and after a brief lull in the mid-1980s, an Elite Eight run in 1989.

The architect of the golden era of Virginia Basketball, Terry Holland, stepped down in 1990, handing the program to a former UVA point guard, Jeff Jones, who would return the program to the Elite Eight in 1995, but ultimately stepped down in 1998 amid a flurry of issues, both personal and those involving lack of success.

Pete Gillen was the hot coach of the moment, but the Gillen Era, which saw UVA rise as high as a Top 5 national ranking in 2002, would not result in a single NCAA Tournament win, and just one tournament appearance, in 2001.

As UVA began construction on a new arena, the John Paul Jones Arena, the program brought on Dave Leitao, a former long-time assistant to UConn coach Jim Calhoun, who had flamed out in a brief run at Northeastern, then had three middling seasons at DePaul.

Leitao did get Virginia back to the NCAA Tournament in his second season, in 2007, and even won a tournament game, but the team missed the 2008 NCAA Tournament, playing in a cable-access-quality postseason tournament called the CBI, and in 2009, after a 10-18 campaign that included a home loss to Liberty, Leitao was gone, in favor of …

Well, not Tubby Smith. The fan base wanted the former Kentucky coach, then at Minnesota, and breathlessly awaited what seemed to be inevitable, in terms of the news that UVA was going to hire a guy who had won a national championship to be its next coach.

That didn't happen, and when it was Bennett who was announced as the guy, the reaction was, honestly, not even mixed.

Bennett had been a head coach for just three years, as far away from the ACC as possible, at Washington State, in the middle of nowhere even in the then-Pac 10.

ZACH PERELES

Bennett had been a national coach of the year, had won 26 games twice, had a 3-2 record in the NCAA Tournament, had been to a Sweet Sixteen, but, OK, Tony Bennett?

Once fans found out that his teams focused on defense, using a system called the Pack-Line that his father, Dick Bennett, had perfected first as a Division III coach, before climbing the coaching ladder all the way to Wisconsin, which he led to the Final Four in 2000, the feeling was, well, great, now we're going to lose, and it's going to be like watching paint dry to watch.

Bennett's first two teams at Virginia struggled as he sold the holdovers from the Leitao regime on what he wanted to do, going 15-16 in 2009-2010 and 16-15 in 2010-2011.

The first, minor, breakthrough came in 2011-2012, when Virginia went 22-10 and got back into the NCAA Tournament, though that season petered out when the 'Hoos lost a promising freshman, Malcolm Brogdon, to a late-season foot injury.

The 2012-2013 team, still without Brogdon, who redshirted as he recovered from the foot injury, seemed certain to be NCAA Tournament-bound into early March, but ended up being left on the wrong side of the bubble, in the NIT, and finished with a 23-12 record.

The 2013-2014 Cavaliers, with Brogdon back, with Harris entering his senior season, with a transfer, Anthony Gill, set to anchor the post, started the season ranked in the preseason polls, but finished non-conference play with an underwhelming 9-4 record, following an 87-52 pantsing at Tennessee.

A meeting initiated by Harris led to a rotation shakeup that put freshman London Perrantes in the starting lineup at the point, and things, suddenly, clicked.

An early January four-point loss at Duke would be the last until a road loss in the regular-season finale at Maryland.

In between, Virginia won 12 straight, and the 16-2 finish in the ACC gave Virginia its second outright ACC regular-season championship in program history.

The 'Hoos would then avenge that loss at Duke in the ACC Tournament championship game, bringing home the school's first tournament title since the Miracle in Landover in 1976.

It had been a blur since. Virginia lapped the field in the hypercompetitive ACC in regular-season play, with an aggregate record of 89-19 over the past six seasons, 10 games better than North Carolina, 12 better than Duke, with four regular-season conference titles and two ACC Tournament titles in that span.

But, one thing missing: that ultimate piece of hardware.

Duke, in the meanwhile, had won the national title in 2015, and North Carolina had won in 2017, after getting to the title game in 2016, and falling on a buzzer-beater to Villanova.

Virginia had not even been to a Final Four under Bennett, despite four 30-win seasons, and four #1 NCAA Tournament seeds.

Then came the UMBC loss, not even arguably the biggest upset in college basketball history, far outshadowing the other biggest upset in college basketball history, also involving Virginia, when a Sampson-led 'Hoos squad lost to NAIA Chaminade in December 1982.

That UVA team would have a chance to recover and go on to the Elite Eight before Sampson's career was cut short by an N.C. State team that would go on to win the 1983 national championship.

The 2018 Cavaliers had a shockingly early start to their postseason training program, then a season of playing road games facing fan bases reminding them in every way imaginable about UMBC.

Adopting the motto "United Pursuit," the team embraced what had happened and turned it into a source of strength, finishing 29-3 after losing to Florida State in the ACC Tournament semifinals, and earning another No. 1 NCAA Tournament seed.

The 'Hoos needed that strength in another pitched battle with a No. 16 seed, trailing Big South champ Gardner-Webb by as many as 14 in the first half, and they were still down six at the half, before taking control early in the second half in what turned into a 15-point win.

A breathtaking stretch followed a classically boring 63-51 win over Oklahoma in the Round of 32. Virginia needed 39:59 to get distance between itself and No. 12 seed Oregon in what became a four-point win that sent the Cavaliers to the Elite Eight.

Then, they had to overcome the Carsen Edwards Show, as the Purdue guard made what felt like had to be every shot he threw at the rim on his way to a 42-point night.

Virginia needed a miracle play in the final seconds of regulation, beginning with a missed free throw by Jerome, freshman point guard Kihei Clark chasing the ball to the other end of the court, finding Mamadi Diakite with a 40-foot laser pass into the lane, then Diakite draining the 10-footer at the buzzer, just to get to overtime.

From there, UVA would go on to win, 80-75, and it was back to the Final Four for the first time since the Reagan Years.

Virginia would blow a 10-point lead with five minutes to go in the national semifinal as Auburn scorched earth with a 14-0 run to go up 61-57 into the final seconds.

Guy hit an off-balance three with 7.4 seconds left to keep hope alive, and then after Jared Harper missed the second of two free throws, Virginia worked the ball up the court, and eventually got the ball back to Guy.

The shot, from three, missed as time expired, and the PA announcer in U.S. Bank Stadium actually called out the final score, *Auburn 62, Virginia 60,* but official James Breeding had called a foul on Auburn guard Samir Doughty on the shot, and Guy had three free throws, with six-tenths of a second on the clock, to send Virginia to the program's first championship game.

He calmly sank the first two, and after Auburn coach Bruce Pearl tried to ice him with a timeout, Guy came back out and drilled the third.

Extending Virginia's stay in Minneapolis an extra two days.

Two agonizingly long, nerve-wracking days for the faithful.

But for the kids, it was no big deal, from the way they were in warmups, basically acting like middle-school kids at whatever resembles shootaround in middle school.

SCOTT RATCLIFFE

There was that one concern, though. Hunter, missing all those shots over Caffaro.

Ah, it was just warmups. Stuff like that doesn't linger to gametime.

If you noticed it at all, you chalked it up to pregame fan nonsense.

Hunter would be fine. Virginia would be fine.

They'd come so far, after all.

## CHAPTER 2
# Planting the seeds

In a cramped locker room in Orlando over two years ago, the Virginia Cavaliers sat dejected and embarrassed, a pool of sweat and offensive misery.

Virginia had just lost to Florida, 65-39. The run was over for a team that was very much in a transition season after losing ACC Player of the Year Malcolm Brogdon and several other standouts from the year before.

But that didn't make this ending any easier. London Perrantes, Virginia's all-time leader in career starts, sat on the bench with tears in his eyes. A magnificent four years had ended with a thud. But as he saw an end for himself, he also saw a beginning for the two youngsters, Ty Jerome and Kyle Guy, learning behind him.

"They're going to have to come back, and if they want to get to that next level, you've got to take this feeling and put the fuels to the fire and get back to work during the summer, during the offseason, so they don't have this feeling again," Perrantes said.

"I know they'll be back."

In Chapter 9 of *The Greatest Salesman in the World*, Og Mandino wrote, "I will love the light for it shows me the way; yet I will love the darkness for it shows me the stars."

In that moment, Virginia was in the dark.

"It's heartbreaking to see London cry," Guy said.

But in that darkness, stars glimmered, even if just faintly. As true freshmen, Jerome and Guy had shown promising signs of becoming top talent in one of the nation's top leagues. Mamadi Diakite, a redshirt freshman, scored a team-high nine points and grabbed six rebounds against the Gators. Jack Salt, then a redshirt sophomore, had eight points and a team-best 10 rebounds.

"Those young guys, Ty and Kyle and Mamadi, as first years, [got] invaluable experiences to play in the ACC and get the amount of minutes they did and the opportunities to get in the NCAA Tournament, ACC Tournament," UVA coach Tony Bennett said. "That's important. It should sting, and that will push those guys to work."

And work they did. That offseason, Guy lost his man bun and added muscle to make him a better scorer inside the three-point arc. Jerome got quicker and stronger in his first college offseason, having missed much of the previous one due to double hip surgery he underwent as a high-school senior.

Diakite continued to grow into a game that was still so new to him. And quietly, a storm was brewing in the background in the form of De'Andre Hunter and Jay Huff, both of whom had redshirted that year.

It was a crucial few months for Bennett, his team and, more importantly, his program. While his players transformed their bodies and their games, his roster transformed as well.

In a two-day span just weeks after the Cavaliers' season ended, Marial Shayok, Darius Thompson and Jarred Reuter announced their intentions to transfer, and they would find homes at Iowa State, Western Kentucky and George Mason, respectively.

Players leaving his program wasn't a new issue for Bennett. Of his six recruits in the well-regarded 2010 recruiting class — the first group he recruited in Charlottesville — four transferred. The two who stayed, Joe Harris and Akil Mitchell, became essential building blocks for the program. And as they helped set the tone for the culture Bennett desired, Virginia basketball grew, too.

Bennett would need a similar effort from those who were still around following the Florida loss. The Cavaliers had become a premier program — a championship contender, even — over the past few seasons, but a second-round loss and the player departures that followed meant that the Cavaliers had work to do to get back to the heights Harris, Brogdon and others had reached.

Sure, veterans such as Devon Hall and Isaiah Wilkins were returning. But the responsibility of righting the ship for both the upcoming season and of upholding program's long-term health rested on the shoulders of that prized 2016 class.

They would not — they could not — disappoint.

One may think Virginia's redemption story — their 38-game journey through the 2018-2019 season that ended with a 85-77 national championship triumph — started after the shocking loss to UMBC last March.

In reality, it started in that locker room in Orlando.

\*\*\*

Something else happened that offseason, though — something much bigger than basketball, much more damaging than any unsightly scoreline.

A Klu Klux Klan-organized rally tore through Charlottesville in August 2017. Three people died. Nearly 40 suffered non-fatal injuries. It was the darkest time for the city the Cavaliers called home, a darkness that, in that moment, had no stars. The Cavaliers would have to create them by themselves.

CRYSTAL GRAHAM

"We came back in the locker room and said, 'How can we fight against that?'" Diakite said. "We're just gonna play hard and lift everyone up and show that the city has more than what people think."

The Cavaliers played hard and played well. They won 23 of their first 24 games, and 18 of those wins came by double digits. They swept Duke and UNC. They reached the top of the AP Poll for the first time in 36 years. They won the ACC regular-season and tournament titles. They earned the No. 1 overall seed in the NCAA Tournament.

Eleven of the 20 wins in ACC play were by double-digits. In five of the games, Virginia never trailed; in three more of the wins, the 'Hoos trailed for 1:38 or less, and in 18 of the 21 conference games Virginia led for at least 24:15 of game time.

Virginia led for 617:47 of its 845 minutes in ACC games, 73.1 percent, and trailed for just 159:17, 18.9 percent.

The loss was to Virginia Tech, by one in overtime, in a game UVA led by five with 30 seconds left, and the Hokies won on a layup off a loose ball with six seconds remaining – and Virginia had a last shot to win both in regulation and the OT.

Six seconds, two last-second misses, from a perfect ACC season.

And then, it was over, in a flash, as the Cavaliers lost to No. 16 seed UMBC, in the first round of the NCAA Tournament.

There's a long list of things that went wrong that Friday night in Charlotte. Hunter and Huff got hurt days before the game. The Cavaliers' normally stout defense got shredded, their normally efficient offense fell off the tracks. They had no answers.

Guy openly wept on the court. Tears filled the eyes of Wilkins. Jerome, one of the team's more emotional players, was too distraught for emotion, monotonously answering postgame questions with a blank stare.

The task for Bennett, after yet another March disappointment, proved one of his toughest.

"[I was] trying to tell the guys in there, 'This is life — it can't define you,'" Bennett said. "You enjoy the good times, and you gotta be able to take the bad times.

"The adulation, the praise, it comes, and we got a lot of that this year. Then on the other side, there'll be blame and people pointing that out. That can't, in the end, define these guys and our team."

Perhaps what he was looking for was the words he spoke in 2016, when his Cavaliers lost a double-digit second-half lead against Syracuse in the Elite Eight: "Weeping may endure for the night, but joy comes in the morning."

Guy and Jerome had to take to the postgame media stage to answer questions, a cruel final twist to a nightmarish night.

"One thing this team is really good at and built on is resiliency," Guy said. "I think bouncing back from something that's so heartbreaking will be a huge key for us."

Even through the puffy eyes and the sorrow-soaked words, Guy was trying to find the joy — to see the stars.

\*\*\*

An April 2018 Facebook post penned by Guy laid bare the emotional maelstrom that players were having to endure in the days and weeks following the defeat, and revealed that even the preternaturally optimistic Guy was having trouble processing what had happened.

"Walking around campus with everyone staring and giving disgusting looks was hard," Guy wrote. "Every person knew my business. Everyone knew our every move. Everyone knows why we were all wearing a hood and headphones. It made me feel claustrophobic, and when privacy is not on the table you begin to be jealous of the freedom of the wind."

Credit to Guy that he didn't write to dwell on the negative. He had come to the point of actually being thankful for the experience.

"I found an appreciation for the light because I've been in the dark," Guy wrote. "After this season, I have been fed and I have starved. We had a fantastic season with lots of accolades and great moments but it ended it in a negative light to most people. For me,

I'm not going to stop the story just because I don't like the scene."

Guy wrote about his emotions as the game unfolded, remembering looking up at the scoreboard at the under-8 media timeout and telling himself to "calm down," then, when Wilkins fouled out with 2:16 to go, going over to Wilkins to say something and finding himself "speechless."

"I realized at that moment that we may not win, but I will not let these seniors, this program, or these fans down. They will remember that I never gave up and I played until that last buzzer sounded," said Guy, who, it is worth noting here, made five of his last six shots from the field, including three driving layups and a tip-in, in the final 5:40, so, yeah, he never gave up.

Guy wrote about having to literally be carried off the court by Hunter, not remembering a word of what Bennett had to say in the postgame huddle in the locker room, then having to face reporters in the press conference while being in a "dark place."

"Last year I tweeted that I never lose, I only learn. That night was the first time I thought I lost in my collegiate career," Guy wrote.

Guy "never hated losing before," seeing it as "a learning process, and it was bigger than basketball, which it absolutely is still both of things, but I now have a profound hate against losing. Every rep and practice requires a type of focus and precision that most people can't reach."

Writing, to Guy, was "therapeutic."

"Not everyone understands the toll athletes go through, and I hope this was a good read for those who don't understand," Guy wrote. "I also hope that anyone struggling in life or sports understands they aren't alone and everyone has a voice to share their journey. You can't judge my story because of the chapter you walked in on. The only way I could continue my story was by putting a bookmark in this chapter and turning the page. See you next year, March."

\*\*\*

Months later, at ACC Operation Basketball, in the same site his season had ended, Guy was ready to get back on the court.

"I think for me, it's never forgetting it, but definitely trying to move past it to where I'm not hanging my head on it," Guy said. "I think it's taken me a little bit longer than some of the other guys, but that's just because I'm an emotional kid, and I'm real passionate about things. That cut me real deep.

"But Coach [Bennett] said something last night when we were meeting with him and Jack, and he said that, you know, courage is not the absence of fear; it's moving forward in the face of fear; and I think that's something that I'm going to hold onto for the rest of my life."

Perhaps this team was able to move forward because they were motivated by the embarrassment, fueled to make a deeper run with the core still intact and, after all, coming off a terrific season.

Or maybe having experienced what had happened in their city the previous summer helped them put things in perspective.

"Let's clarify something," Bennett said. "I've been through the worst, basketball-wise, OK? Let's keep this in perspective."

\*\*\*

Virginia, until last year, had been synonymous with March disappointment because they had not broken through to the Final Four.

But they had never gone through something like the UMBC loss. For a second straight year, the Cavaliers had to push themselves even harder. There was no other way. That renewed dedication took many shapes.

Jerome met with Bennett three days after the loss to discuss offensive changes and hoisted jumpers in JPJ until he was kicked out of the gym. Guy opened up about his issues with anxiety on social media and through letters. Hunter spurned a possible leap to the NBA because he thought Virginia could do bigger and better things with him healthy. Diakite admitted he was "ashamed," which drove him to new heights.

Simply put, everyone surrounding the Virginia program made changes to get better. To move on. To make sure Virginia basketball had bigger and better things coming its way.

The team motto, "United Pursuit," was more than just words. If they were to weep together, they were to find joy together. If they were to go through the darkness together, they were to emerge into the light together. Bennett is a diligent and studious man, always searching for a new quotes, new philosophies and new ideas. One he settled on for the 2018-2019 campaign was simple: "The joy is in the competition."

As the Cavaliers climbed toward the light, they embraced that competition. In August, Bennett took the team whitewater rafting in West Virginia. For those few days, there was no on-court work to be done, no drills to finish, no game plans to solve. There were competitions — a mini-golf tournament and rafting races among them — but there was camaraderie.

"I learned to trust [my teammates and coaches]," Diakite said. "I felt like we were syncing with the coaches. The coaches looked sort of like players. We could interact and have fun. That hierarchy wasn't here. We were just playing around."

Of course, whitewater rafting isn't for the faint of heart. For as confident as Hunter and Diakite were on the court, they were equally as intimidated by the roaring waters of the New River Gorge.

Diakite still doesn't like jumping into murky water. If he can't see the bottom, he doesn't want to go in.

It's a reasonable apprehension. He doesn't want to be, as he put it, "surprised."

Bennett, frankly, didn't care.

"Coach Bennett went under the water and grabbed my leg." Diakite said. "I screamed. I didn't know what he was. Then he said, 'I got you!'"

There were plenty of reasons for the Virginia basketball team to venture out into the water and out of the players' comfort zones.

The first and foremost one?

"Because it's a blast," Bennett said with a smile. "Have you ever been whitewater rafting? I mean, come on. And some of our guys were scared to death, so it was even more fun to watch them be scared to death. It was the highest point of the rapids, and ... our guys' eyes were big. We had to beg [Hunter]. 'It's going to be OK.' But, no, we just wanted to have a blast."

Hunter didn't quite see it that way.

"I was just glad I was alive," he said.

In the middle of all the chaos — of the raft races and the scared faces and the new places — Bennett found himself, if just for a few moments, contemplating what lay ahead. It wasn't the next set of rapids or the trip back to Charlottesville. It was the season as a whole.

"I remember just like it was the most beautiful setting just floating down the river with these guys, and I remember saying that in my mind," Bennett said. "'I'm floating on that river. What's this year going to bring?' Because it's a significant year, I thought that. I was thinking, 'Wow, here I am.'"

And there was Virginia, just a group of college kids and their coaches, managers, trainers and other staffers, laughing and swimming and rafting and screaming their way through the early-August heat.

Some overcame fears. Others didn't. But in those few days, Virginia drew closer as a team. There is no doubting that.

Their road was just starting.

\*\*\*

Braxton Key remembers the text he received in Greek Art History class. He remembers the exact feeling of his heart rate jumping.

The Alabama transfer had chosen Virginia as his new home in early May. By mid-June, he had petitioned for a hardship waiver, which would give him immediate eligibility and allow him to bypass the redshirt year typically required of undergraduate transfers.

But it was late October, and he still hadn't received a decision from the NCAA.

Would he join a team that looked to contend for a national title? Or would he have to wait a year, unable to participate in the game he had been hooked on for so much of his life?

The text from Bennett simply told him to call after class.

Key had waited for months. He'd have to wait another few minutes before finding out his fate. The clock couldn't have gone slower.

That's what made the good news all the sweeter. The NCAA had granted Key's waiver. He'd be suiting up with his fellow Cavaliers for the season opener in just two weeks.

"Honestly, in my mind, I thought I was going to be playing all

JOHN MARKON

year," Key said at the team's media day. "I just kind of was trying to speak good things into the universe and just see where it would go from there.

"The guys around here have been great — Kyle, Ty, Dre have been picking me up and saying, 'You may be able to play this year, you may not. But just, if you are going to play, you might want to practice in case you're gonna play.'"

At 6-foot-8 and 225 pounds, Key brought the physical skills you can't teach. He combined that terrific quickness, strength and physicality for his size, and he could rebound with the best of them. He was ready-made for the Pack-Line defense — such a natural fit that he had almost committed to it a few years earlier.

"Really close," Key said when asked about possibly committing to UVA originally. "I mean, they were in my top four. I wasn't able to take a visit. I really wanted to, but [Hunter] committed the week I was supposed to take a visit."

Two years later, he was able to start his college career anew at the place he had almost ended up out of basketball factory Oak Hill. Key had been a top-100 recruit, and his production at Alabama — 9.8 points and 5.5 rebounds — offered a glimpse of what he could do. He was a proven quantity at the high-major level.

Kihei Clark, on the other hand, was anything but. The 5-foot-9 three-star recruit out of Woodland Hills, Calif., had been committed to UC-Davis before a standout summer between his junior and senior year.

Clark showed his terrific on-ball defense on the Nike EYBL circuit, where the best prep players in the nation play their AAU ball. On the other end, he was a poised facilitator who proved unfazed by bigger or stronger competition.

Bennett, a former undersized guard who had to rely on smarts himself, could appreciate that. The Virginia head man came calling, and Clark appreciated how he was made a priority, even late in the recruiting cycle. The Cavaliers secured a commitment, even as hometown UCLA came sniffing around.

Would Clark redshirt? It's not easy for an undersized guard to adapt to the rigors of college basketball at any level — much less in a conference such as the ACC — and succeed right away. But Bennett needed just one moment to know his faith in Clark would be rewarded.

In one summer practice, Jerome, fresh off a standout performance at NBA All Star Chris Paul's CP3 Elite Guard Camp,

JON GOLDEN

grew so frustrated with Clark's dogged full-court defense that he hurled a ball toward Clark's head.

If Clark could rattle Jerome, he could rattle — and therefore play against — anyone.

"He'll definitely add a lot to our defense," Jerome said before the season. "His energy — to our defense and our offense, really — during whatever his role is this year will be tremendous for us."

Bennett, meanwhile, immediately found an apt comparison.

"I played against Muggsy Bogues, so I know about somebody who is up under you and can always be a problem," Bennett said.

Bogues, at 5-foot-3, is the shortest player in NBA history. Clark was only a year old when Bogues retired, so he hadn't exactly idolized the journeyman point guard growing up. Still, he knew the role could fit him perfectly.

"I definitely know who he was, and I know how he played," Clark said. "[Bogues] was a bulldog on the ball, and he didn't back down from anybody, so I kind of had to implement that into my game as well."

The other two newcomers were international products Kody Stattmann (Australia) and Francisco Caffaro (Argentina). Both were long-term projects.

Stattmann, an outstanding shooter on the wing, needed to add muscle and adjust to the speed of the American game. Caffaro, an exciting down-the-road prospect, averaging 16.7 points and 8.8 rebounds a game in the FIBA U18 Americas Championship in June, earning all-tournament status at the event alongside four five-star recruits, would redshirt to deal with injuries and learn from the veterans — Salt, Diakite and Huff — in front of him.

So, Virginia was set. With Key and Clark prepared to join the rotation, the Cavaliers looked to not only have solid depth but outstanding versatility.

Bennett could match basketball's latest fad, the four-guard lineup, by playing Clark, Guy, Jerome and Hunter together with Diakite.

That group could provide quickness, athleticism, outside shooting and scoring.

But if the Cavaliers needed a bit more length and rebounding prowess, he could add Key into the mix. Against a particularly physical team, Salt would answer the bell with his thunderous screens and strong interior defense. And when needed, Huff, who was recovering from a torn labrum, would grow into his role as a three-point-shooting, dunk-stuffing, shot-blocking machine, providing valuable minutes at crucial junctures.

The Cavaliers had the personnel to be one of the best teams in the nation. They had the experience of the previous year to fuel them. They had heard the four letters "UMBC" enough.

For the Virginia Cavaliers, it was time to start the season of redemption — to become the team of destiny.

# CHAPTER 3
# The last unbeaten team

Tony Bennett tends to like to schedule light for his openers, to let his teams ease into the season.

It allows for slow starts, like was the case in the Nov. 6 season opener against Towson. It took a while for the Cavaliers to get on track, but eventually, what was supposed to happen happened, as Virginia blitzed the Tigers, who would go on to a 10-22 finish in 2018-2019, by a 73-42 count.

Ty Jerome had 20 points, and De'Andre Hunter had 13 points and 10 rebounds.

Braxton Key started his first game as a 'Hoo, and Kihei Clark was the first man off the bench, scoring four

JOHN MARKON

points and contributing hounding defense in 24 minutes.

It was your typical Virginia season opener, though. Virginia led just 28-19 at the break, shooting 37 percent (10-of-27) over the opening 20 minutes.

"We were sort of shuffling around on the offensive end early, either lost our balance, couple dead plays, but then I did think we picked it up for the most part positionally and rebounded a little better, and again took some stands defensively," said Bennett, who, despite his best efforts, had to address the elephant in the room, in the form of UMBC.

His childhood friend, Erich Bacher, the sports information director for the basketball program, had the TV in the media room postgame tuned to UMBC's season opener with Marquette.

"I want to thank Bach for putting the UMBC game on for me in my postgame press conference," Bennett said, drawing laughter from the press corps. "That's really great of our sports information director."

Marquette, which would spend a good portion of the 2018-2019 season in the Top 10 before a late-season fade, led by 13 at the break and went on to an easy 67-42 win over the Retrievers in that one.

The early-season blahs continued with a middling effort in a 76-57 win over George Washington in Game 2 had Bennett reinserting his starters late, to send a message to his team.

It was message received in Game 3, a 97-40 win over Coppin State, in rebuilding mode under former Maryland star Juan Dixon, in a game that was never in doubt.

Then it was on to the Bahamas for the 'Hoos, in a tournament billed as Battle 4 Atlantis.

The field looked competitive: among the teams on the island were Wisconsin, which would earn a No. 5 seed in the NCAA Tournament on Selection Sunday; Florida, a No. 10 seed that would advance to the second round of the NCAA Tourney; and Oklahoma, which would meet up with UVA in the second round of the NCAA Tournament.

Virginia didn't end up facing off with Oklahoma in the Bahamas, defeating Middle Tennessee by 74-52 in the opening round, struggling for most of the game in what turned into a 66-59 win over Dayton, which would finish 21-12 and lose in the first round of the NIT in March, then winning the title-game matchup with Wisconsin, 53-46.

That Wisconsin game, played as most of Wahoo Nation had its focus on the UVA-Virginia Tech football game in Blacksburg on Black Friday, marked a pivotal moment for the 2018-2019 Virginia basketball team.

Clark got his first start of the season in the win, logging 37 minutes, scoring five points, recording three steals and two assists, with Key getting just 12 minutes off the bench.

Clark got the start on the road at Maryland in the ACC/Big Ten Challenge, getting 35 minutes in the 76-71 win that would prove to be significant later on, in the context of the NCAA Tournament wins for the 'Hoos over Purdue and then, in the national championship game, over Texas Tech.

Virginia was known for beating opponents with its defense, but Maryland, by and large, shredded the Pack-Line, shooting 54 percent.

"We tried to make adjustments there, I think Jack [Salt] challenged himself, and other guys did, and we tightened our pack defense," Bennett said afterward. "We thought that was important that guys guarded on the ball better. I thought Kihei [Clark] made some defensive slides that were real big and [the Terrapins] hit some tough shots at the end, but it was enough."

The Cavaliers came home with the win with offensive efficiency, scoring 1.267 points per possession, hitting 10-of-22 from three-point range, and balanced scoring, with five players in double figures.

Also key: just two turnovers.

"We took care of the ball — I want to emphasize that — because they can get out and run," Bennett said.

\*\*\*

The win at Maryland finished November for Virginia at a 7-0 mark, with two wins over Big Ten teams that would go on to earn NCAA bids.

The 'Hoos opened December with an easy 83-45 win over Morgan State. Next up was VCU, which was on its way to a 25-8 finish, an Atlantic 10 regular-season title and NCAA Tournament appearance.

The Rams gave the Cavaliers everything they could, leading by five with seven minutes left on a snowy Sunday, before Virginia closed on a 19-6 run to pull out the 57-49 win.

UVA won despite shooting just 29.5 percent from the floor, so, pretty much the polar opposite of its win over Maryland a couple of weeks earlier.

This one would also be significant. Think of the ugly win over Oregon in the Sweet Sixteen.

"I am OK with it, especially with the way the offense needs to work today, when you needed to use the dribble because of how aggressive they were," Bennett said after the VCU win. "We just kind of stuck with what we did, a couple of little things here and there to try and toughen up offensively."

JOHN MARKON

One moment from the second half would end up on the season highlight reel, for what happened on the court, and on the sidelines.

Clark, playing with a cast covering a broken left wrist suffered in the Morgan State game, suffocated VCU's P.J. Byrd with what amounted to a one-man full-court press, forcing a 10-second-call turnover that keyed the game-closing run.

The play brought the crowd at the John Paul Jones Arena to its feet, including in that number, Bennett.

The coach leaped skyward and quickly sought out Clark amidst the madness of the moment.

"That was the most amped I've ever seen [Bennett]," Jerome said after his 14 points (eight of them coming during the endgame run) helped the Cavaliers improve to 9-0. "[VCU] was trying to bring the ball up the court and call timeout, but the kid [Byrd] couldn't even get to half-court to call it. That's how good of a job Kihei does on the ball."

The broken wrist would actually require surgery the next day, and after the VCU game, Bennett was noncommittal on when Clark might be able to return.

The 10-day exam break helped, but shockingly, Clark was back on the court for Virginia's next game, on the road at South Carolina.

Clark was the first player off the bench and logged 24 minutes in the 69-52 win in Colonial Life Arena, which, not coincidentally, would host first- and second-round NCAA Tournament action in March.

What, you don't assume that Bennett scheduled this game without having thought that through, because you know better than that, right?

South Carolina, at the time, was struggling through a rash of injuries, but the Gamecocks would finish 16-16, 11-7 in the SEC, with a home win over an Auburn team that Virginia would meet in April in Minneapolis.

But that was a ways off. As far as December was concerned, the Virginia team had to find a hotel in Columbia, and then had some time to get used to the locker rooms, the sidelines and the sightlines in Colonial Life Arena, which had to be a help later on, when the Cavaliers would get their assignment on Selection Sunday.

\*\*\*

UVA finished out December with easy non-conference wins over William & Mary and Marshall, the latter of which, on Dec. 31, saw the 'Hoos score 100 – yes, 100, as in, 100 points, in a single game.

The Marshall win was the 300th for Bennett in his career, including his time at Virginia and at Washington State.

"I'm thankful," Bennett said after the game. "It just means I have really

good players. It means I've been coaching for a while. I've had a great staff. My whole hope is that, in my 300 wins, I've honored and respected the game, the people who've poured into my life and what I value as important, and that in the many games I've lost, I've done the same."

That one was also just about the oddest game you'll see a Virginia team play in terms of tempo. Marshall isn't quite Loyola-Marymount from the early 1990s, but the Thundering Herd did play tempo to its advantage, for the most part, averaging 74.3 possessions per game, fifth-most in the nation, according to KenPom.com.

The Virginia game actually saw the tempo play to Marshall's favor, with each team recording 76 possessions in the New Year's Eve tilt.

As good as the offense was — the Cavaliers shot 53 percent from the field and 44.4 percent from Bonusphere — the defense was just as good. UVA held Marshall to 35 percent shooting (20-of-57 from the field) and 27 percent behind the arc (6-of-22), while holding Herd star Jon Elmore to his worst game of the season (3-of-17 from the field, and 1-of-8 from the arc) for 14 points (seven of those coming from the free-throw line).

As with the earlier win at Maryland, this was a sign that this wasn't your father's Tony Bennett Virginia Cavaliers team.

The 2018-2019 'Hoos could beat you 53-46, could beat you 76-71, and could outrun an up-tempo team that would go on to win 23 games, as Marshall did, on its way to winning the CollegeInsider.com Tournament, defeating Bennett's alma mater, Wisconsin-Green Bay, by a 90-70 margin in the final.

\*\*\*

Virginia wrapped the nonconference portion of its schedule with a 12-0 mark, but it didn't feel like there was as much in terms of tests as you might have thought when you saw the schedule ahead of the season.

Marshall had won 25 games and advanced to the Round of 32 in the NCAA Tournament in 2018, for instance, but didn't sniff the bubble in 2019.

Middle Tennessee, similarly, had won 25 games, and had been left out of the NCAA Tournament, controversially, in 2018, but the Blue Raiders limped home to an 11-21 finish in 2018-2019.

There were three wins over teams that would compete in the 2019 NCAA Tournament – Wisconsin, Maryland and VCU – but, for comparison, Duke had already beaten Kentucky, which would advance to the Elite Eight; Auburn, which Virginia would face in the Final Four; and Texas Tech, who the 'Hoos would face in the NCAA Tournament final.

The ACC opener for Virginia, on Jan. 5, against Florida State, which had advanced to the Elite Eight in 2018, and already owned wins over eventual SEC regular-season champ LSU and Elite Eight participant Purdue, brought with it the threat of a bit of comeuppance.

There was, indeed, comeuppance in the offing.

For Florida State.

\*\*\*

Key had a career game for the Cavaliers, scoring 20 on 7-of-11 shooting, and UVA broke open a close game with a 15-2 run to close out the first half in what turned into a 65-52 win.

"My teammates had confidence in me, and I had confidence in myself, so

JON GOLDEN

just whenever I had any open look, I just tried to be a little bit more aggressive today than normal, and the shots were falling for me today," said Key, for whom the 20-point effort was a season-high.

Jerome and Hunter, who each came in averaging 14 points a game, combined for just 12 points (each had six) on 4-for-19 shooting.

Kyle Guy, in the process, set a Virginia record of making 11 straight three-pointers, carrying over from the Marshall game (last six in a row) on New Year's Eve until Saturday (first five in a row).

Against the Seminoles, Guy scored a game-high 21 points, including 5-of-6 from behind the arc and 7-for-11 overall from the field.

Over that two-game stretch, Guy scored 51 points (shooting 12-of-15 on three-pointers).

"You know, you watch him play on film, and you just don't believe a guy is capable of being that confident when he shoots the ball," FSU coach Leonard Hamilton said, shaking his head almost in disbelief.

"I'm not sure I've seen many guys that seem to feel as good wherever they are on the floor that they're capable of putting it in the basket ... and he does. We just didn't have any answer."

The 'Hoos held the Seminoles' top three scorers — Terance Mann, Mfiondu Kabengele and Trent Forrest — to a combined six points on 2-for-12 shooting.

Mann, who averaged a team-high 13.1 points a game coming in, did not score and missed his only two shots in 18-plus minutes off the bench.

Next up was Boston College, which hung around with Virginia for a half, before losing 83-56, with Mamadi Diakite being the offensive stalwart in Chestnut Hill, scoring 18 points on 9-of-12 shooting.

UVA shot 60 percent (33-of-55) in the midweek win, and then it was back on the road for a Saturday-afternoon tilt at Clemson, which happened to be hosting a celebration for its new national championship football team on campus that morning.

The occasion would be remembered later by Bennett at another championship celebration held in a football stadium.

\*\*\*

"We're riding up on the bus, and it was the time they were gonna celebrate the football national championship," Bennett said at the April 13 UVA basketball championship celebration at Scott Stadium.

"And we're riding up on the bus, and the stadium's full, and we're getting ready for our game, and I remember thinking, 'Man, what would that be like if we ever won a national championship?'"

First things first. Clemson, a Sweet Sixteen team in 2018, rode the emotional energy in Littlejohn Coliseum as the team, struggling at the time, at 10-5 on the season, looked to pull the upset.

A Marcquise Reed layup cut the Virginia margin to two with 17:23 to play, but the 'Hoos outscored the Tigers 21-5 over the next seven minutes, then coasted to a 63-43 win.

The man of the hour offensively was Jay Huff, who scored 11 points on 4-of-5 shooting in 10 minutes off the bench.

It was Huff's first career ACC double-digit scoring game, and one that he hoped would be a harbinger of things to come.

"I think it hopefully will lead to more opportunities," Huff said. "I've always believed in myself — I thought I could've played in some of these games — but I always wanted to learn from Mamadi [Diakite] and Jack [Salt], and I think I've tried to learn from them as best I can, so thanks to them for teaching me."

The win lifted Virginia to a 15-0 start.

Looming: a rematch, of sorts, in JPJ with No. 9 Virginia Tech.

\*\*\*

Virginia was now ranked No. 1 in the country. In February 2018, a UVA team on the verge of a No. 1 national ranking faced a Virginia Tech team that had crafty coach Buzz Williams devising an interesting game plan.

Williams schemed his team into a 61-60 overtime win by going with a pack-it-in zone that had all five Hokie defenders with a foot in the paint, taking Virginia completely out of its motion offense, and forcing the 'Hoos into hoisting an absurd 38 three-point shots, knocking down only 11 of them.

It was the only home loss of the 2017-2018 season for UVA, and also the only ACC loss.

The 2018-2019 Hokies spent a fair amount of time ranked in the Top 10 of the national polls, and would end their season a layup at the buzzer away from taking Duke into overtime in the Sweet Sixteen.

They had their own projected early-entrant lottery pick, Nickeil Alexander-Walker, and two really, really good college players, rim-running point guard Justin Robinson and center Kerry Blackshear.

JOHN MARKON

Williams had been building toward this season for five years, after posting an 11-22 mark in 2014-2015, the first season of the rebuild, going 20-15 and getting the Hokies into the NIT in 2015-2016, then beginning a stretch of back-to-back-to-back NCAA Tournament appearances in 2016-2017.

Williams also had the distinction of being able to say that, at least of late, he was more than holding his own in head-to-head matchups with Bennett, notching a win over the 'Hoos in each of the past three seasons.

Williams seemed to have a foresense of what was about to happen this time around.

"I think [Virginia] was good enough to win the national championship last year, and I think they're good enough to win the national championship this year," Williams said in a conference call with reporters on the eve of the in-state matchup.

"I think they're running more stuff than they've ever run since I've been at Virginia Tech," Williams continued. "A much wider [offensive] catalogue. They have more offensive weapons, they're playing more personnel groupings than in years past, and I think that's why their play catalogue is larger. They're doing it with more versatility."

That versatility was on display from the outset. Virginia shot 68 percent from the floor in the first half, went into the break up 44-22, and never looked back in an 81-59 win.

"It's a little bit of pick your poison, because I don't think that there is ever necessarily a non-shooter or a non-offensive player on the floor [for Virginia]," said Williams after the game. "I think [UVA] is incredibly sound in what they do.

"They are doing more than they have done in the past," Williams added. "I think [Bennett] utilizes that talent in different ways, but there is not a guy that they are going to put on the floor that can't make shots or make a play for one another."

The Hokies entered the game leading the nation in defensive three-point field goal percentage. They gave up 10 – count 'em, 10 – three-pointers in the first half.

"Defensively, you're stressed from the start," Williams said.

He was correct in that assessment. Virginia's three-headed monster of Guy, Jerome, and Hunter, combined to shoot 18-of-31 for the night.

But that wasn't all. Key had seven points on 3-for-5 shooting; Huff was 3-for-3 from the floor with a made three; Clark, who regained his shooting touch after having his cast removed the day before the game, made three of his six shots, all three of his buckets being from behind the arc.

Pick your poison, indeed.

One of the overlooked intangibles in this game didn't have anything to do with statistics. Many believed that in the loss to Tech a season earlier, the Hokies came in and took it to the Cavaliers from the get-go.

Not in this one. Virginia was wire-to-wire jacked up and was ready to meet any intensity the Hokies may have packed for the trip.

"We punched them in the mouth early and didn't let off the gas pedal," said Guy, who finished with 15 points.

It was the second time in 10 days that the Cavaliers annihilated the ninth-ranked team in the nation. (Florida State was the first).

When reminded of that fact, Bennett, in his modest aw-shucks way of blowing off his team's dominance, commented about well his team had played and shot the ball, and defended well, before he said what it all means.

"Your reward is you get to go to Duke next," Bennett deadpanned.

# CHAPTER 4
# Mirror images

Duke and Virginia went into the Saturday mid-January clash ranked at the top of a national poll (Duke in the AP, UVA in the coaches).

Both were built around Big Threes; both with talented supporting casts.

Both were ranked in the KenPom.com top five in terms of adjusted offensive efficiency; both were also ranked in the KenPom.com top five in terms of adjusted defensive efficiency.

One difference: the guy coaching the young guys was older (Mike Krzyzewski, 71); the guy coaching the older guys was younger (Tony Bennett, 49).

Another: the younger coach has an old soul. Virginia played the nation's slowest pace, averaging 60.7 offensive possessions per game, 353rd, and dead last, nationally.

Duke averaged 75.6 offensive possessions per game, seventh nationally.

That's the old guy, adopting the new style: pushing pace.

Tempo is how two teams that are statistically similar in every other way can play to disparate average scores.

Duke was outscoring its opponents on average 90.3-66.9.

Virginia's average score: 74.3-51.7.

Both played essentially position-less eight-man rotations.

Bennett would not blink at subbing out 6-foot-10 center Jack Salt for 5-foot-9 point guard Kihei Clark.

Krzyzewski could go big with 6-foot-11 Marques Bolden and 6-foot-10 Javin DeLaurier or spread the floor with three-point shooters Alex O'Connell and Jack White.

But the focal points were the Big Threes, all of whom will be playing at the next level.

You knew already (thanks, ESPN!) about Zion Williamson, R.J. Barrett and to a lesser extent Cam Reddish.

Williamson was the beast in the post at 6-foot-7, 285. Barrett was the

6-foot-7 slasher/scorer, and Reddish a silky smooth 6-foot-8 perimeter threat.

Virginia's power troika was 6-foot-2 Kyle Guy, Ty Jerome at 6-foot-5 getting into the lane for teardrops and kickouts, and 6-foot-7 De'Andre Hunter a threat in the post and dribble-drives.

They could all score. They could all defend – each of the six were rated in the top 20 in the ACC in defensive rating.

It really was like looking in a mirror, just that the images on the one side moved a little faster.

The matchup was as much chess match as it was a basketball game.

First, you know going in that you don't approach Williamson defensively with a single guy. No such guy – a Shutdown Zion Williamson Guy – exists, not in college, not in the NBA.

You don't stop Zion Williamson, as the saying goes: you only hope to contain him.

What you were to see, you supposed, would depend a bit on how Krzyzewski approached his Tre Jones problem.

Jones, a freshman point guard, had gone down to injury in Duke's 95-91 overtime home loss to Syracuse earlier in the week. Coach K would play coy with the issue of whether or not Jones would play, but ultimately, Jones would be in dress clothes.

To account for Jones' absence, then, would Krzyzewski go big – with Bolden and DeLaurier surrounding his Big Three? Or spread the floor – going with three-point guys White and O'Connell?

How would Bennett counter, lineup-wise? Would Hunter start out on Williamson, to try to take away Williamson's dribble-drive game, make him one-dimensional, in the post, with help when he got the ball in the post from post-to-post doubles from Salt or Mamadi Diakite?

Might Diakite get some defensive possessions on Williamson against the Duke big lineup? Hunter could hold his own against either DeLaurier or Bolden in the post, and going that route, you'd force Duke to recognize the switch and run a set for Williamson to get the ball on the wing.

You basically tell Diakite in this setting, sag, give him space for a jump shot, let Williamson be a jump shooter, then close out.

You could try Salt, but, no, actually, maybe you don't try Salt. That just invites a clear-out and an ESPN highlight.

If Duke went small, if you can call White at 6-foot-7 and O'Connell at 6-foot-6, alongside Williamson, Barrett and Reddish going small, the best defensive lineup might be Guy, Jerome, Hunter, Diakite and Braxton Key.

Then on the flip side, what does Duke do defensively, without Jones, its best on-ball defender? Might you see Coach K sprinkle in some zone to try to steal some minutes with a shortened bench?

The possibilities seemed endless.

\*\*\*

Williamson and Barrett combined for 57 Duke points as the Blue Devils held on to give Virginia its first loss of the season in a 72-70 barnburner.

The Blue Devils grabbed a lead early on with the help of offensive rebounds and stickbacks, and stayed on top until halftime, but never led by more than seven in the first half.

Duke had nine offensive rebounds over the opening 20 minutes, which translated into 11 second-chance points as UVA trailed 37-32 at the half.

Virginia shot 58 percent from the field prior to the break, but connected on just 1-of-8 from long-range.

Williamson and Barrett each posted 14 points in the first half.

The 'Hoos took their first lead since the first media timeout on a pair of Key free throws with exactly 14 minutes left in the game. From that point on, the lead changed hands 11 times as the teams went blow-for-blow.

Jerome hit a floater in the lane with 9:50 to play, and the Cavaliers went on to miss 11 of their next 12 shots from the field, but managed to stay within three points or less during that stretch — until a late Duke flurry swung the momentum with time winding down.

Barrett split a pair from the stripe to give Duke the lead for good, 55-54, with 8:36 to go. Up by one, Barrett scored on a tough bucket to make it 63-60 with just over three minutes to play.

Guy had a wide-open look at a three to tie it up on the ensuing trip, but couldn't connect, and then Barrett scored Duke's sixth consecutive make with 2:18 left.

Jerome missed a long three on Virginia's next possession, and then Hunter had a layup roll around the rim and out with a little more than a minute to go.

Barrett, who misfired on four freebies earlier in the game, went 4-for-4 from the line in the final minute and gave Duke a 69-61 lead with 44 seconds left.

Key dunked one home with 37 ticks showing to pull the Cavaliers back to within two possessions, then Guy nailed an open triple after two free-throw misses by Williamson on the other end, and UVA was down by just three, 69-66, with 23 seconds remaining.

Barrett and Key traded pairs of free throws to make it 71-68 with eight seconds left.

Reddish made his first free throw to make it a two-possession game but missed the second, and Hunter knocked down a jumper on the final scramble just as the final horn sounded.

"I told our guys in the locker room that it wasn't our effort," Bennett said. "We had our chances, but 63 percent [Duke's field goal percentage the second half] ... we weren't solid enough. Credit [Duke's] play and ability, but we have to be better than that."

Williamson bulled his way through Virginia's Pack-Line for 27 points (on 10-of-16 shooting) and drew numerous fouls from myriad of Cavaliers trying to guard him. He was 7-of-14 at the free-throw line.

Coupled with Barrett's game-high 30 points (11-of-19), Duke was hard to stop.

Those two Blue Devils combined for 57 points and 21 made field goals, while the rest of the Duke team scored 15 points and contributed five made field goals.

Virginia, which came into the game leading the ACC three-point field goal percentage at 46.3 (its nearest competitor was Louisville at 37.7), suffered its worst shooting night from behind the arc since league play began earlier in the month, a mere 3-for-17 (a season-low 17.6 percent).

The Blue Devils did it with defense, switching on screens from one through five, something Duke hadn't done to that point in the season.

The switching gave the Devils a size advantage at every position.

"We felt that we could not defend [Virginia's] baseline floppy curls," Krzyzewski said. "They're so good. Guy is the closest that I've seen to J.J. [Reddick] in this league. Not saying he's J.J., but he's close. A lot of people can't shoot turning, but he can.

"So, we just said we're going to try to limit their open threes, and we did a really good job of that with the switching," Krzyzewski added. "We got beat sometimes on the handle, but they're two-pointers."

As a counter, Bennett tried to spread the floor more and attack Duke's middle, a strategy that worked well with Guy, Jerome, and Hunter driving the lane and scoring effectively.

"Yeah, their defense put up a lot of pressure, but it was easier to go by [them] because they were so stretched out," Guy confirmed. "I think we probably should have taken a little more advantage of that instead of calling a lot of ball screens and trying to run off screens. A lot of our points came when we got in the lane."

In fact, Duke only outscored UVA in the paint, 46-42, in spite of the Devils' size dominance.

While Guy and Jerome said they wished they could take some of the missed three-pointers back (they were a combined 3-for-12), they were not discouraged.

"What was the score, 72-70?" Jerome asked. "We usually win when we score 70. The offense was definitely not the problem. We missed shots we normally make.

"We'll see them again at home," Jerome added, with a twinkle in his eyes. "We had that game. We lost it. We made mistakes that we can control."

\*\*\*

JOHN MARKON

The ACC helped Virginia with scheduling after the first Duke game.

Wake Forest was the comedown game for the 'Hoos, at home, three nights later, and the Cavaliers opened the game on a 25-3 run and coasted to a 68-45 win.

Next up was a game in South Bend at Notre Dame, in an uncharacteristically down year for the Fighting Irish, which were on their way to a 14-19 finish.

Notre Dame had won the ACC Tournament, with a 32-6 record and Elite Eight appearance, in 2014-2015, and had gone back to the Elite Eight in 2015-2016, but had missed the NCAA Tournament in 2017-2018, and the cupboard was bare this season, as coach Mike Brey was trying to develop a young team on the fly.

UVA opened this one with a 23-7 lead halfway through the first half, on its way to a 17-point halftime edge, and it was not really close from the opening tip onward.

The end of the quick two-game road swing, at then-No. 23 N.C. State, would be a tougher-than-expected test, as Jerome suffered a back injury early, and struggled in trying to play through it, with four turnovers.

Guy, meanwhile, though perfectly healthy, still had struggles of his own, shooting just 3-of-11 from the floor, though he made his only three of the night count, draining a jumper from the right corner to give Virginia the lead for good with 1:59 to go in overtime in a 66-65 win.

State finished with 16 offensive rebounds, five by bullish Wyatt Walker, who was so strong that he moved Salt off the block a couple of times.

Virginia, which led the nation in fewest turnovers per game with an average of only 8.4 coming into Raleigh, doubled that number.

"We played well enough to win, but a couple of those stats stick out," Bennett said afterward. "N.C. State plays good defense. They're good with their hands, they're athletic, they're aggressive, and they did rattle us and take us out of our rhythm.

"Usually when you give up that many offensive rebounds and that many turnovers, you're not going to be successful," Bennett added. "We need to grow from this and learn from it. We brought losing into the equation when I didn't know we had to in certain situations with fouls and turnovers and unsound decisions."

One game remained before Virginia would get its rematch with Duke, with a week off in between the Feb. 2 game with Miami and the Feb. 9 game with the Blue Devils, both at JPJ.

Jerome would miss the Miami game with the back injury. Clark started at the point in his place, doing some good things (scoring nine points on 3-of-6 shooting, dishing out six assists) and some bad (six turnovers in 37 minutes) in the 56-46 win.

"At times, early on, we got some good looks out of our ball-screen offense, and we just missed a lot of shots," Bennett said. "That seemed like it was the best chance to have an

JON GOLDEN

opportunity to get some scores. We were struggling in some of our other stuff, so we just tried to ride that a little more and be as good as we can offensively.

"But that showed at times, the indecisiveness, that led to some turnovers and either forced shots or not making the right plays. Again, there were enough good plays, and that is part of learning."

Virginia was now 20-1, 8-1 in the ACC, and, for a week, the attention was on Duke, Part II.

\*\*\*

According to the ticket reseller SeatGeek, the Duke-UVA rematch was the hottest home hoops ticket at JPJ since SeatGeek began tracking the secondary market in 2010.

The average resale price was at $304 a ticket the day before the game, nearly three times the average for a UVA home game in 2018-2019.

The rematch was also a hot TV ticket, with the *ESPN GameDay* crew on hand to mark the occasion, the fourth *GameDay* visit to JPJ in five years.

Jay Bilas offered a quick thought in a meeting with local reporters as UVA went through a walk-through on the eve of the game as to the interest of *GameDay* in Virginia basketball.

"They win," said Bilas, who played for Duke from 1982-1986 and has been part of *GameDay* since its inception in 2005. "We go places that win, because those are the highest-rated games. People want to see a winning team. The last five, six years, they've been as good as anybody and as consistent as anybody."

Seth Greenberg, who coached against Bennett for three seasons while at Virginia Tech, was singing his former rival's praises in the meetup with the local media.

"He's the same guy in a disappointing loss to UMBC as he is a great win against Duke and winning an ACC championship," Greenberg said. "I think the consistency of his approach and his consistency of how he communicates with his team and coaches his team is the reason that you see the product you see. He's a phenomenal teacher and terrific tactician, but … you can't be all those things if you're not a great communicator.

"He understands exactly who he is and how he wins, and he's not going to deviate, and he's not going to take any shortcuts in the kind of guys he wants in this program, and he's going to develop to guys he has to get them to play the way he wants them to play."

Greenberg wrapped by bringing up the notion that the logical next step for Virginia was a national championship, and that he had no doubt in his mind that Bennett could achieve that, citing Virginia's ACC success as support.

"They're playing teams that are winning championships and competing for championships," Greenberg said. "If the system's good enough to beat those teams, it's good enough to win a national championship."

\*\*\*

Jones was back at the point for Duke after missing the first matchup, and Jerome, after sitting out the Miami game, was in the starting lineup for Virginia.

With NBA superstar LeBron James among those in attendance, Duke started out blazing hot, hitting its first five threes, and never trailed en route to an 81-71 win.

Emblematic of the night for the Blue Devils, a 30.8 percent three-point shooting team: Barrett, a 31.4 percent shooter this season from three-point range, hit five of his first six bombs, and finished 6-of-10.

Reddish, a 34 percent shooter from three coming in, was 5-of-8.

It was that kind of night for Duke.

For UVA, it was a night of playing from behind. Duke led 8-0, 19-9 and 29-15, but Virginia closed to 39-35 at the half.

The Blue Devils opened the second half on a 12-6 run to get the margin back to double digits.

The 'Hoos would twice get the margin to five, the final time on a Hunter three with 5:25 left, but Duke had the answer each time.

Duke shot 57.8 percent from the floor (26-of-45), and was led by Barrett's 26 points (8-of-15 FG).

Williamson had 18 points on 6-of-8 shooting. Reddish had 17 (6-of-10 shooting).

Virginia shot 46.7 percent from the field (28-of-60) and 10-of-24 (41.7 percent) from three-point range.

Guy and Jerome each had 16 points. Guy shot 6-of-15 from the floor and was 3-of-9 from three-point range. Jerome was 6-of-11 from the floor and 2-of-5 on threes.

Duke was 13-of-21 from long-range.

A 30.8 percent three-point shooting team shot 61.9 percent from three.

"When they hit 13 threes, they are going to be hard to beat," Guy said.

Virginia must have felt the sky was falling. The Cavaliers played well. They shot 47 percent, outscored Duke in the paint, outrebounded the Blue Devils. Just couldn't stop the rain of terror.

Duke posted the highest shooting percentage from the field against Virginia since 2010, when Washington connected on 58 percent of its shots in an overwhelming win over the Cavaliers on the road.

"We tried to keep Duke out of the lane and jam the lane," Bennett said. "We probably over-corrected in terms of that."

The Cavaliers were slow on closing out, leaving their man and racing out to harass shooters at the arc. They didn't get their hands up when they weren't late.

"But we did jam the lane, so we had that going for us," Bennett half-joked.

The good news was that it took what felt like an act of God, with Duke going absolutely bonkers from three, to win by 10.

Duke shoots its season average from three, and it loses by 10.

It wasn't anything Duke did, anything Krzyzewski did, as even the great Coach K conceded after the game.

"I don't think it's anything I did, but my players felt it," Krzyzewski said. "Maybe that little room, they took advantage of it without any kind of coaching. Really good players make coaches look pretty good, pretty smart."

Good players who can't shoot threes who suddenly make a ton of threes. Fixed that for you, Coach K.

But, again, that was the good news, that it took something that wouldn't happen again for Duke in 2018-2019 to beat Virginia on this night.

The bad news: it was the second different way that Duke had beaten Virginia in 2018-2019.

First time, in Durham, it was dribble-drives to the lane and finishes at the rim.

Second time, it was hitting threes when Virginia took away the driving lanes.

It seemed inevitable that these two would meet at least one more time in 2018-2019. That's how clear it seemed that Duke and Virginia were head and shoulders the best two teams in the country, no matter what the rankings had to say about the matter.

Duke had Virginia's number. That much was obvious.

Compounding things in the immediate term for UVA was the loss of Diakite, who scored seven points in 10 first-half minutes, but left after he collided heads with Hunter as both tracked a loose ball and didn't return, and was reportedly feeling "foggy" on the bench and afterward.

Which would be significant, because as helpful as the ACC office was the first time around the schedule, giving Virginia games with second-division conference foes Wake Forest and Notre Dame to get back into the swing of things, it was payback time the second time through.

In less than 48 hours, UVA would face North Carolina, winners of 11 of its last 12, in Chapel Hill, on Big Monday.

# CHAPTER 5
# Duke in the rear-view

The North Carolina Tar Heels had almost gotten caught in their trap game against Miami, needing a late Luke Maye three to force OT, then having to hold on to beat the 'Canes, 88-85, hours before Virginia's home loss to Duke.

To be fair, then, you'd have to point out that both teams had the short turnaround heading into their Big Monday clash.

Though, OK, North Carolina had the second-division Hurricanes at home, early in the afternoon.

Meaning: the Tar Heels were in Chapel Hill, with time to rest, recover, watch film, have a walk-through, shootaround, pretty much on a normal schedule.

Virginia, on its side, had a night game, and a road trip to make, after having spent a week getting ready for Duke.

Meaning: yeah, not a lot of time to get ready for a team that was looking like a national championship contender.

The pressure was on Francesco Badocchi.

Wait … Francesco Badocchi?

\*\*\*

The Sunday between the Duke and UNC games, the associate AD for basketball administration/operations, Ronnie Wideman, approached the redshirt freshman guard, and accomplished pianist, to ask if he could be the point man for a game of "Name That Tune."

Badocchi remembered later that he'd been asked to learn "like, 10 songs," for the occasion, which was a play on something he had done to help loosen the team up on road trips – performing for his teammates and coaches in hotels that had a piano.

Walk-on Jayden Nixon would emerge over time as the go-to "Name That

JON GOLDEN

Tune" guy among the players, and Bennett was the clear favorite among the coaches, Badocchi said.

"I played some oldies, and [Bennett] got most of those," Badocchi said.

The "Name That Tune" stratagem worked as Bennett had hoped it would, according to Ty Jerome.

"I think it was because we wanted to get off our feet more, because that Carolina game, we were coming off Duke two days before," Jerome said with a smile. "So, they wanted us to get off our feet as much as possible and get as much rest, and Frankie started playing the piano, and he's so talented in that. I think Coach [Bennett] just selfishly wants to hear him play."

Bennett has long preached the "joy of competition," and that included competition as lighthearted as "Name That Tune," which became a staple of pre-game prep.

From that day forward, Badocchi would have advance notice — best case, a night or two before, but sometimes, just a few hours — to start preparing his songs.

Badocchi logged a total of 28 minutes on the floor in the 2018-2019 season. His most important minutes came on the piano keys.

\*\*\*

Virginia led 36-29 at the half, but a 17-3 Carolina run over a 5:39 stretch turned things around for the Heels, who would eventually lead 55-48 on a Maye turnaround jumper with 7:51 to go.

But the tide was already turning, even with the Maye jumper giving UNC its biggest lead of the night.

It happened during the under-12 media timeout.

Bennett threw a rare hissy fit, and the timing couldn't have been any better.

During a timeout, the mild-mannered Virginia coach unleashed on his team. For the fourth game in a row, they had committed double-digit turnovers, atypical of how the Cavaliers had performed in the previous 19 games, when they led the nation in fewest miscues per game (8.4).

The Tar Heels were scoring off UVA turnovers, getting easy baskets, and on the verge of handing the Wahoos back-to-back losses for the first time since 2016-2017 (to Duke and UNC).

To that point, Virginia had committed 10 turnovers, prompting Bennett to lose his cool.

"[Assistant coach Brad] Soderberg said [afterward], 'I'm glad you channeled your inner Dick Bennett' [Tony's father, a former coach]," Bennett laughed in his postgame chat. "Obviously, we had struggled with that the previous three games, and I just said, 'Enough's enough.' I really challenged them. I barked at 'em."

Meanwhile, Jerome was busy telling his teammates to calm down, that everything was OK, that Virginia is built for this sort of situation.

"[Carolina] went up six and made a run, and [Bennett] started losing it," said Jerome. "I think he started screaming, and I tried to keep everybody calm and take care of the ball down the stretch."

Jerome's words resonated with his teammates. Virginia didn't commit another turnover the rest of the game, stormed back to knot the game at

59-all with four minutes to play, then bested Carolina 10-2 the rest of the way, including two long-distance daggers by Kyle Guy.

The yelling was just part of the story, though. There was some strategy in that under-12 huddle as well.

Bennett had started Kihei Clark at point, the thinking there being, Clark, a solid on-ball defender, would give Carolina point guard Coby White fits.

Clark, looking at the box score, played 27 minutes, but then looking at the play by play, he subbed out at the 11:32 second-half media timeout, and didn't return.

Meaning: Bennett decided that his thinking going in about Clark on White wasn't working.

White, to that stage, had 15 points in the game, shooting 6-of-12 from the floor, 3-of-7 from three-point range, with one assist and two turnovers.

Not working at all, is a better way to put it.

As Bennett was yelling at his team during the media timeout, he was subbing Guy and De'Andre Hunter back in, for Clark and Jack Salt.

Hunter, at 6-foot-7, was put on White, at 6-foot-5, the idea now being, you have to assume, that Hunter's length would give White trouble, after 27 minutes of being able to see over the 5-foot-9 Clark.

Virginia trailed 49-43 at the 11:32 mark. Again, White had the 15 points, was shooting 6-of-12.

With Hunter as the primary defender on him the rest of the way, White would score just two more points, on a pair of free throws at the 9:25 mark, and miss his last seven shots from the floor, four of them from three.

North Carolina had scored 20 points on 8-of-14 shooting in the first 8:28 of the second half, up to that 11:32 media timeout.

The Tar Heels would score just 12 on 4-of-20 shooting in the final 11:32.

White being neutralized was one key factor there.

The rotation was pared from eight to six at the 11:32 media timeout, and that Clark had subbed out, as had Salt.

Salt wouldn't return, either, as Bennett went with Mamadi Diakite and Jay Huff at the five in a four-guard lineup, alongside Hunter, Guy, Jerome and Braxton Key.

Diakite and Huff essentially split the minutes in the post, but of note is that Huff was on the floor for the game's most important stretch.

The 7-foot-1 redshirt sophomore subbed in for Diakite at the 6:52 mark, with UVA still down 55-51.

Which is to say, the first chess move by Bennett, putting Hunter as the primary defender on White, had slowed UNC's roll, limiting the Heels to six points in that stretch of 5:40, but the margin was still at four.

Huff would play the next 5:54, subbing out for Diakite with 58 seconds left, and Virginia up 67-61.

That's a 16-6 'Hoos run over that 5:54.

Huff only scored two points over that stretch, with a single defensive rebound, and a steal.

The bucket turned out to be the one that would put UVA ahead to stay, a layup on a dish from Hunter with 3:12 to go, on a nice dive to the hoop when Huff's defender went to double Hunter on a dribble-drive to the rim.

You could argue that Huff just happened to be on the floor while good things were going on around him, but games involving two Top 10 teams and coaches the level of Tony Bennett and Roy Williams don't turn on things just happening.

Huff's unique skillset on the offensive end draws attention even when he isn't hitting shots. He's the rare seven-footer who is a threat from three and off the dribble, and as such has to be accounted for on the offensive end in a way that Salt, whose range goes out to about three feet, give or take, can never bring to that side of the floor.

Where Huff has had to earn his minutes has been on the defensive end.

The Virginia Pack-Line is predicated on help, and breaks down if all five guys on the floor aren't doing their part.

Huff was on the floor to dive to the rim on the Hunter dribble penetration because he was doing his part on the defensive end to justify Bennett having him out there.

UNC scored six points in that nearly six-minute stretch as UVA's offense started to click with Huff part of that mix.

Bennett had found himself another contributor, in what players and coaches would later call the team's biggest win of the regular season.

It would also be UNC's last regular-season loss, as the Tar Heels would go on to sweep Duke and finish 16-2 in the ACC, tying Virginia for the regular-season title, even cutting down the nets after completing the sweep of the Blue Devils on the final Saturday of the regular season.

Virginia would cut nets down on that Saturday as well, and the ceremony at John Paul Jones Arena felt a little more real than the one in the Dean E. Smith Center, because of the 69-61 Cavaliers win on this Monday night in February.

\*\*\*

The next game, with Notre Dame, offered a chance at a breather, on paper.

Virginia had easily dispatched the Fighting Irish, 82-55, in South Bend in January.

Notre Dame coach Mike Brey had a wrinkle for the back end of the home-and-home: a 2-3 zone.

What the hay, right? Brey was playing with a depleted roster, and what he'd tried in South Bend hadn't worked.

Brey kept his team in the 2-3 until the final seconds in what turned into a 60-54 loss, in a game that was tight into the final seconds.

"I thought we defended well. We really guarded them. We're certainly offensive challenged, so we're going to have to guard. I thought we really defended them well," said Brey after the game, in which his Irish held Virginia to 36.5 percent shooting.

The issue was the kind of shots that UVA took, or rather, settled for.

Most glaring: the 23 threes, representing 44.2 percent of the Cavaliers' shots from the floor.

On the season to this point, 37.1 percent of Virginia's shots had come from three.

Next: Virginia was just 4-of-7 on shots at the rim – layups or dunks.

What that works out to is 13.5 percent of Virginia's shots coming at the rim.

The season number: 36.6 percent.

What you get, then, is a lot of two-point jumpers, the shots that the analytics people say are bad, because they're from further out, they tend to be contested, and if they go in, they're only worth the same that a layup or dunk.

Quick math had 42.3 percent of Virginia's shots against Notre Dame being two-point jumpers.

Season average: 26.3 percent.

UVA shot 7-of-22 (31.8 percent) on those shots against Notre Dame.

Season average: 37.3 percent.

So, Virginia shot a lot more jumpers, in general, more threes, in particular, a lot more contested twos, and didn't shoot as well on the jumpers.

This was the case in the last 10 minutes at Duke, it was the case game-long in the loss last season to Virginia Tech.

How you attack it is how Virginia tried to attack it Saturday. You put somebody in the middle of the zone, in the area of the free-throw line, and try to go at the 2-3 from that soft spot.

UVA used Hunter primarily in that role, and his numbers – 6-of-11 shooting, getting to the foul line for seven attempts, two assists, no turnovers – would suggest that he did about as well as you could expect.

Jerome, unfortunately, was almost completely neutralized. Jerome finished with eight points, but was just 2-of-9 from the field, and significantly, was 0-of-6 on two-point shots.

Jerome is at his best breaking down defenders on dribble-drives, touching the paint, hitting that teardrop jumper, and then when the opponent sags off to try to take that away, using the sliver of space he gets to drain open threes.

JOHN MARKON

Against the Notre Dame zone, Jerome seemed content to drift around the perimeter, making him so much less effective in terms of being a scorer, and he also didn't have much impact in terms of assists.

Jerome had 11 assists (against two turnovers) in 37 minutes in Virginia's 68-61 win at North Carolina on Monday.

Against Notre Dame, Jerome had three assists, and three turnovers, in 36 minutes.

You could bet that opposing coaches scheming ways to beat Virginia in March would look at this game tape and see a weakness.

***

A ferocious putback dunk, a mini pull-up on the rim, a big smile and a slight flex toward his own bench, with a point to his flexed bicep included.

That was all Guy needed to shock — and then incense — the Hokie faithful inside Cassell Coliseum.

"It felt great," Guy said after the game, a 64-58 Virginia win. "You can let a lot of frustration out when you're that high in the air."

Guy was adamant that it wasn't his first putback dunk, but minutes later, Jerome deadpanned, "That's a first."

Key, though, came to Guy's rescue. The two had faced each other in AAU ball, and Guy was a big part in bringing Key, a transfer from Alabama, to Charlottesville. So, he would know as well as anyone if it was indeed Guy's first putback jam.

"He had an All-American game in Rucker Park, and he had about six dunks," Key said. "That's his glory days. ... That's the last one I remember."

But the minutes previous to the dunk were ones Guy would like to forget. Virginia Tech scored on its first four possessions, including two easy buckets from Ahmed Hill, Guy's defensive assignment.

"We were switching off ball defensively, which we don't do," Bennett said. "They ran good fake screens and slips, but we were just out of position. ... I didn't understand a couple of things that took place, and that's why I took him out. It wasn't just him — it was kind of everybody, and we needed to get it right."

So, Bennett pulled his leading scorer out at the first dead ball. His players needed to get it right, and that started with Guy.

It worked to perfection for the junior guard.

"He just said that I just gotta in my stance and be a little bit more alert," Guy said. "It helped me refocus to know that we've just got to play through that."

He came back in 75 seconds later and poured in 14 more points — in addition to an early three — to give him 17 for the half, more than half of his team's total output of 32. It was a shooting performance that, for all intents and purposes, saved Virginia's then-fledgling offense.

Given the Cavaliers' struggles through the first 20 minutes — they turned the ball over eight times and allowed five offensive rebounds — their 32-29 advantage wasn't just a bit of luck, but also a testament to Guy's scorching offensive game.

"What [Coach Bennett] said to us at halftime, it was kind of hard to remember we were up," Jerome said. "He really gave it to us. We were definitely fortunate to be up three the way we were playing."

The visitors also made it to halftime in the lead despite missing Hunter for much of the half. He was forced to sit for the final 12 minutes of the half due to two early fouls.

"Whenever he's in foul trouble — or Ty or me — the other [two] of us three have to be a little bit more assertive, a little bit more aggressive," Guy said. "We're always looking for our shots, but when someone's out, the offense can get stagnant at times, so we just try to move the ball and get open looks."

Guy was indeed aggressive, pulling the trigger 10 times in the opening half and connecting on six shots, including four threes.

The long balls rained in from everywhere. The corner. The wing. Up top. One even banked in from an impossible angle.

"I didn't know that one was going in," Guy said sheepishly. "Part of being a good shooter is just shooting the ball with confidence, and I know I can get hot at any moment, so when my teammates are feeding me, I'll keep shooting."

The Cavaliers played considerably better on both ends in the second half. Virginia Tech shot 11 percent from three in the contest, the Hokies' worst shooting performance from deep since 2016. And the Cavaliers made them pay time and time again.

When Key splashed down a triple with 5:51 remaining to stretch the Cavaliers' lead to 13, Virginia Tech called a timeout, and the wind fell out of the sails of a once-raucous Cassell Coliseum.

Key, who had made just one three in the past month and had missed his first three attempts of the night in Blacksburg, was finally on the board.

The Cavaliers weren't at the finish line yet, but they were close. Jerome embraced Key after Buzz Williams called for time.

"He missed one the play before that … and he had his head down walking back," Jerome said. "I told him, 'Keep shooting. If it comes in, and it comes down and you're open, you've got to let it go. Shoot with confidence. I believe in you.'"

It was a big moment for the player and the team. Key said he's been taking hundreds of extra threes to get back on track.

"He said, 'I told you,'" Key said. "He's been telling me, 'Stick with it. It's gonna fall. Your moment's gonna come.' It's been rough for the past couple games, for sure, but you've just got to stick with it, and it finally happened. It was a good feeling."

A few members of the maroon-clad crowd picked up their coats, waved goodbye and left their hopes at the door after the Key swish.

It looked for a moment that they may have made a massive mistake. The Hokies cut it to seven points with 2:32 to go, but that was as close as they would get until an uncontested layup by Nickeil Alexander-Walker with four seconds left provided the final margin.

As it turned out, the most important thing they missed was another three from Guy — his sixth of the night — to put the game out of reach.

It was nothing those who had departed early hadn't seen already.

# CHAPTER 6
# Winning the ACC again

The last visit to Louisville had worked out, in the end, for Virginia.

The 'Hoos had trailed in the 2018 game in the KFC Yum! Center most of the night by double-digits, but Ty Jerome, down four, with nine-tenths of a second left, was fouled on a three, which, no, that made no sense, that first thing.

Neither did Virginia getting the ball back after Jerome intentionally missed the third free throw, and the Cavaliers had lost possession on a lane violation.

Deng Adel traveled on the inbounds giving the ball back to Virginia.

No sense, that.

You almost never see that happen.

Then De'Andre Hunter banked in a three at the buzzer.

Bonkers.

Virginia trailed by four with nine-tenths of a second left, and won, in regulation.

The Cardiac Cavs were back in Louisville, and fell behind by double digits again at the end of a wild first half in which it seemed that the Cardinals couldn't miss.

Louisville was 10-of-16 from three on its way to a 37-27 lead at the break.

The ending wouldn't be anywhere near as dramatic as the game a season ago, but it did have to do with Hunter.

Hunter, as in the win earlier in the week at Virginia Tech, was relegated to the bench early in the first half with two fouls, this time having been whistled for back-to-back personal fouls within 30 seconds.

It's a Tony Bennett rule that, two fouls in the first half, you sit, no questions asked, and so it was that Hunter had to sit there and watch as his teammates were getting torched.

"That's super frustrating, one of the worst feelings, because you know you're going to have to sit for the rest of the half and can't help your team," said Hunter's best friend and teammate, Jerome. "I know what Dre was going through.

"When he came out for the second half, he looked a little mad," Jerome said.

Mad, indeed.

Hunter came back with a controlled rage, a fury unleashed on Louisville, and the Cardinals didn't know what hit 'em.

Hunter scored a then-career-high 26 points, 19 of those in the second half, making all six of his shots from the field, to key the 64-52 win.

It was his most complete performance on both ends of the floor, in advance of the national-title game.

Hunter was dominant on offense, and he shut down Louisville star Jordan Nwora, who after scoring 12 points — including a pair of big three-pointers — in the first half, was silenced in the second, handcuffed by Hunter's smothering D.

Louisville's top scorer was held to five points after the break, shooting only 2-for-9 overall, 1-for-5 from beyond the arc.

Virginia needed the very best of Hunter, and it got just that.

He simply took over the game.

"He's multi-talented, he's smart, he lets the game come to him, but also stays aggressive, so he has a feel that some scorers don't have," Jerome said. "He never forces, but just naturally scores. Today, he dominated the game."

Hunter, who is a modest sort, kind of admitted his dominance afterward, but in a very humbling manner.

"I just get a little mad," he said about sitting out most of the first half. "I just want to be out there, so when I get a chance, I just want to be aggressive.

"When I make my shots like that [second half], I was feeling good and wanted to keep shooting, and my teammates kept feeding me the ball," Hunter said.

Bennett and Hunter's teammates see it every day in practice.

"He's just continuing to evolve his game," Bennett said of Hunter. "You can see it. He's improving. He's just playing at a high level.

"In practice, he shows signs of that, but to do it in games is a little different, when we need it and there are other really good players on the floor," Bennett explained. "When he's on the floor, he's a matchup problem, just like when Nwora at the four is a matchup problem. That's the way the game is kind of going."

This time, no miraculous deeds were required of Hunter, who still remembered being buried under a human dogpile of celebrating teammates after hitting the winning basket a year earlier.

"I thought about it when we walked back in [the building]," Hunter said of the shot. "I thought about how we celebrated in the locker room, but this is a different year, a different game."

Bennett preferred it this way.

"That was so improbable last year," the coach said. "This one was the way you're supposed to come back."

In doing so, UVA continued its dominance over Louisville, having now reeled off eight consecutive wins over the Cardinals, including four in a row in this building.

There would be two more to add to the wins in the building list in a few weeks, including one that might surpass the 2018 last-second win in terms of drama.

***

Virginia closed out February with an easy 81-51 win over Georgia Tech back in the John Paul Jones Arena.

The win clinched a double-bye in the upcoming ACC Tournament for the 'Hoos, who improved to 13-2 in the ACC.

"That's a great accomplishment, and we're thankful for that," Jerome said. "You never want to take anything for granted. We worked really hard to [secure a top-four seed], so we're thankful for that, but we have such a long way to go, so much better to get. So, we just have to keep working."

Quote of the night came from Georgia Tech coach Josh Pastner, asked postgame his thoughts on whether this Virginia team was national championship material.

"Probably, maybe the odds-on favorite to do it," Pastner said.

Another big win over a second-division team would follow. Virginia defeated Pitt, 73-49, to open March.

The Cavaliers took control of this one with an early 16-0 run, leading 39-19 at the break, allowing Bennett, prepping for another Saturday-Monday, on the road at Syracuse on Big Monday, to limit minutes for his starters down the stretch.

"We'll play on Monday, our third game in however many hours or days, so [the starters] did the job early and to start the second half," Bennett said. "It was a way to also reward the guys who work hard in practice. So, of course, to do be able to do that was important."

***

Virginia had posted a 5-1 record in regular-season games against Syracuse since the Orange had joined the ACC in 2013-2014.

There was that one loss in the postseason that still stung.

'Cuse rallied from a double-digit deficit in the Elite Eight in 2016 to defeat UVA 68-62, keeping Bennett from his first Final Four.

What Jim Boeheim teams do well seems to match up well with what Tony Bennett teams do well. Boeheim's 2-3 zone takes a team that prefers to run motion out of its game; Bennett's Mover-Blocker offense is, in essence, a motion offense.

The offensive approach for Boeheim teams is heavy on iso ball, with multiple guys who can break down defenders off the dribble and get to the rim, and if help comes, the wings have guys who can shoot threes; Bennett's Pack-Line is predicated on help, and is oriented toward forcing the ball from the paint to the perimeter for lower-percentage shots from behind the arc.

For a half in the Carrier Dome on this last Big Monday of the season, things were working in Boeheim's favor, with the Orange leading 34-32 going into the break.

Then Boeheim, the Hall of Famer, who has been coaching at Syracuse forever, saw something he'd never witnessed before.

"They shot the ball as good as I've ever seen it shot," said Boeheim, who has coached at Syracuse either as an assistant or head coach since 1969. "They didn't just make easy, wide-open [threes]. They made some wide-open threes, but they made about six of them from six, seven feet behind the line. There aren't that many teams, if any, that can make those kinds of shots."

The Cavaliers shot 18-of-25 from three-point range, tying the UVA program record (2007 vs. Gonzaga), while establishing a new school mark for triples in an ACC game.

In fact, the 18 makes from behind the arc were the most ever in an ACC game under the present three-point line distance of 20-feet, 9-inches.

Syracuse's game plan was to make the Cavaliers, who entered the game as the nation's fourth-best three-point shooting team, to drive the ball and get UVA off the three-point line.

Instead, Kyle Guy, Jerome, and Hunter turned the Carrier Dome into their personal shooting gallery. The Wahoo trio finished with a combined 18-for-23 from three-point range and beyond. One of Jerome's deep threes came from just a pace inside the block "S" at midcourt.

Guy drilled in a career-high eight three-pointers (second most in UVA history: Curtis Staples, nine) and led Virginia with 25 points. Hunter added a career-high five threes (21 points), and Jerome finished with five threes (16 points), and a career-high 14 assists (tied the school record).

Guy was most lethal, scorching the nets on 8-of-10 shots from behind the line.

"When you let Guy and Jerome shoot those shots, they're going to make them," Boeheim said. "They just took over."

Indeed.

The Cavaliers actually trailed 43-42 with 15 minutes remaining when they torched Boeheim's celebrated 2-3 zone from the perimeter during a 27-3 run. Virginia made seven three-pointers during that point flurry that left Syracuse stunned.

"[Virginia] just took over and dominated the game in the second half," Boeheim said. "They shot it well, and their defense was better. We had no answers for it."

Indeed, as Boeheim alluded to there, Virginia wasn't only impressive offensively. The Cavaliers picked up their defense after the break and left Syracuse flat.

The Orange was 7-of-26 from the field in the second half (27 percent) and were 3-for-12 from three-point range.

"I have a lot of respect for Virginia," Boeheim said. "It's probably their best team that I have seen by a lot. They're really good. They have a great chance to be a national championship-type team."

\*\*\*

A win over Louisville in JPJ on the final Saturday of the regular season, and Virginia would win its fourth regular-season ACC title in the past six seasons.

It wouldn't come easy.

Louisville, trailing by three at the half, opened the final 20 minutes with a 14-4 run that put the Cardinals up seven with 16:16 to go.

It would be a slog from there. Back-to-back threes by Guy and Braxton Key put UVA back in front, 61-59, with 6:23 to go, but Christen Cunningham answered with an and-one on Louisville's next possession, the free throw putting the Cardinals on top, 62-61.

JOHN MARKON

An 11-2 Virginia run over the next 5:30 would put it away. Louisville shot just 2-of-11 from the floor in the final 5:45 as the Cavaliers took control on their way to a 73-68 win.

A Jay Huff three-pointer, his third of the game, put Virginia up 66-62 with 5:10 to go, and the score would get no closer.

UVA struggled a bit at the line trying to close it out, shooting just 5-of-8 from the charity stripe in the final 1:11, but it didn't matter.

In the 64-52 win at Louisville two weeks ago, it was the Hunter show, as the

JOHN MARKON

redshirt sophomore scored 26 points on 9-of-11 shooting.

Hunter struggled in the rematch, shooting just 3-of-13 from the floor on his way to scoring nine points, but Jerome more than made up for it.

Jerome had scored just four points on 2-of-12 shooting in the win at Louisville, but in the second matchup, the junior carried the team, scoring 24 points on 8-of-14 shooting with a game-high six assists in 39 minutes.

It was the final home game for redshirt senior Jack Salt, the lone senior, and old man, of the group.

"I think we've made the joke he's been here 17 years at least a hundred times this year," Guy wise-cracked. "He's big on the court, off the court. He's a really good dude and has a weird accent."

Everybody owns their own Salt impression, but Guy probably does the best of the big New Zealander who hails from Auckland.

The kidding aside, his teammates have nothing but respect for the big guy, who is a member of the New Zealand national team, the All Whites (white and black are the country's official colors).

"This year Jack has been asked to do something not many people are asked to do," said Jerome. "Going into a game, he doesn't know how many minutes he's going to get, or if he's even going to take one shot during the game, and his attitude never changes.

"He'll give 110 percent for us every single possession, and that's something you don't see in almost any other guy in the country," Jerome said. "If you ask them to take 30 minutes one game and five minutes the next, I don't know any other guy in the nation that would give you their all, and he does.

"He continues to lead every day. He continues to fight through back pain. He's just, he's a warrior, and I'll go to battle with him any day."

Salt would only log 11 minutes and didn't score in the win, missing both his shots and pulling down just one rebound.

He wasn't a factor in his home finale, but he'd be key in Charlotte.

\*\*\*

JOHN MARKON

Charlotte. Where the bad thing had happened.

The Spectrum Center, the host to the 2019 ACC Tournament, had been the scene of the crime in 2018, the first-round NCAA Tournament loss to UMBC.

In a way, it was like they'd never left. Half the arenas the Cavaliers played in, there were always jokers sporting UMBC basketball jerseys, students chanting "UMBC!"

"Everybody says you're going back to Charlotte where you lost to UMBC," Bennett said in a pre-ACC Tournament presser. "We've tried to grow as much as we can and learn from it."

The quarterfinal opponent would be N.C. State, which seemed to have wrapped up an NCAA Tournament bid with a come-from-behind win over Clemson a day earlier.

State, remember, was the team that gave Virginia the most trouble that it had faced outside of its two losses to Duke in the ACC season, taking the Cavaliers to overtime before losing 66-65.

The Wolfpack led by four early in the second half in a game that felt oddly like the loss to UMBC in 2018.

N.C. State was getting all the loose balls, making the big shots, and the Cavaliers seemed to be waiting for somebody to step up.

In the UMBC loss, nobody answered the call.

Salt would have none of that this time around.

Salt registered a career-high 18 points and grabbed six rebounds as Virginia overcame the slow start in the 76-56 win.

In his 119 career games leading up to this one, Salt, a career 3.2-point-per-game scorer, had given most of his offensive contributions as an off-ball screening machine. But with his team down 31-27 early in the second half, Salt took matters into his own hands.

He tracked down a long offensive rebound, turned toward the basket, took one hard left-handed dribble, two more steps and put up a reverse layup through contact from N.C. State's Wyatt Walker.

Salt stumbled all the way to the opposite sideline as the ball bounced high off the rim and settled into the net.

Count the bucket, and the foul. The Virginia bench erupted.

Salt knocked down the ensuing free throw. Virginia was within one.

"I got the board, and he was expecting me to pass it, because that's what I usually do when I get an offensive rebound, but I just ripped, and it was there, and then had the up-and-under," Salt said.

"That was nuts," Huff deadpanned.

In a vacuum, it didn't look like that would be the moment that swung the game. In fact, Wolfpack guard Markell Johnson nailed a tough three-pointer on the other end to restore his team's four-point lead.

Rather, it proved to be a sign to come for the Virginia big man. A few possessions later, with Virginia trailing 34-32, Salt rolled to the rim off a screen, caught a perfect bounce from Jerome and finished again with a foul. A career 44-percent foul shooter, Salt knocked down another free throw (he finished 4-of-5 from the line) to give the Cavaliers a 35-34 lead, their first since halfway through the first half.

Buoyed by Salt's scoring spurt — he had eight of Virginia's first 10 points coming out of halftime — the Cavaliers didn't look back. After taking a 37-36 lead on yet another Salt putback a few trips later, Virginia never trailed again, outscoring the Wolfpack 39-20.

Upholding his reputation as a giver, Salt, who scored 15 points in the second half, directed the praise toward his teammates.

"My teammates [were] finding me wide open," Salt said. "[N.C. State's players] were extending on help, and [my teammates] were being guarded by my man, so they were just finding me, and I was getting easy looks at the rim."

\*\*\*

Duke, which had been without freshman star Zion Williamson for three weeks, with a knee injury sustained in the opening seconds of the Blue Devils' loss to North Carolina in the first game of their home-and-home, got their guy back, and with Zion, Duke, which had gone 3-3 and needed luck to beat lowly Wake Forest at home a week before, was suddenly, again, the Best Team That Anybody Had Ever Seen.

The Blue Devils outlasted Syracuse in their quarterfinal matchup, setting up a third straight year of Duke-UNC in the ACC Tournament semifinals, with the Tar Heels having dispatched Louisville in their quarterfinal tete a tete.

Virginia, quietly, on the other side of the bracket, which might as well have been the other side of the galaxy, would face Florida State, which had won 13 of its last 14 games, including a thrilling 65-63 OT victory over Virginia Tech in its quarterfinal game.

UVA had blown the doors off the Seminoles in Charlottesville back in the teams' ACC opener way back in early January, but that seemed an eternity ago at this stage.

It was a very different FSU team on the floor in the Spectrum Center in the Friday night lead-in to Duke-UNC.

SCOTT RATCLIFFE

Florida State led for 38 minutes and 14 seconds, and dominated the battle of the boards, 35-20. Reserve senior guard David Nichols, who came in averaging 6.3 points a game, scored eight of his game-high 14 points during a crucial 13-1 run midway through the second half after UVA cut it to one point, 49-48, on a Jerome stepback three-pointer at the 12-minute mark.

Every time the Wahoos started to chip away, FSU had an answer. To make matters worse for Bennett's bunch, seemingly every loose ball down the stretch bounced into the hands of the Seminoles.

Bennett admitted afterwards that the 'Noles were the better squad on this particular night.

"We had some chances to win the game, I think we went up [one point]," Bennett recalled, "but Florida State played well, they defended well, they were sound, and tonight they were the tougher team, or more physical, they're physical that way.

"So, we look at the things we can clean up, and you always have a growth mindset, that's the way it is."

Florida State won, 69-59, and Virginia was on a plane heading back to Charlottesville, awaiting its next destination on Selection Sunday.

Which, hey, was something to look forward to.

There was still basketball to play.

The last time Virginia lost a game in Charlotte, that was it, season over.

"I wanted these guys so bad to get a chance at a title fight, but that didn't happen," Bennett said. "It wasn't that their effort was poor or anything, but now we'll use it to our advantage."

Asked if he subscribed to the theory that taking a loss at this stage of the season might bring everything into focus for his team, Bennett responded immediately.

"I do now," he quipped. "All right, we lost, we'll get some extra rest for these guys, we'll grow, learn from the tape, and you take the hand that's dealt, and make the most of it."

# CHAPTER 7
# Return trip to Columbia

Five points. Five fouls. Twenty minutes.

Those were the combined numbers from Mamadi Diakite in two games at the ACC Tournament. They weren't pretty.

Even uglier, though, was the result of the Cavaliers' time in Charlotte. After dominating an N.C. State team that would go on to miss the NCAA Tournament, Virginia fell 69-59 to a long, athletic Florida State team.

The loss looked too much like failures of March past for these Cavaliers. Their initial game plan didn't work, their opponent kept hitting tough shots, and they quickly ran out of options.

They panicked. They lost.

Diakite, who had blossomed into Virginia's go-to big man thanks to his quickness, leaping ability and versatile defense, mostly just sat on the bench and watched. In another one-and-done tournament setting, his team was yet again done earlier than they had envisioned.

But this wasn't going to be like last year. It couldn't be. Especially not if Diakite had anything to say about it.

"What I know is, no matter how much you fail, if you get up and keep fighting, you can have good results," Diakite said. "That's what we're trying to prove to everyone. It doesn't matter if you lose against a 16 seed or whoever. Just keep doing you. Keep fighting. Come back again. Try again."

So, Diakite did try again. But he also tried something new. After two performances that simply didn't reflect all the progress he had made over the course of the regular season, he requested a meeting with Tony Bennett.

The exact words were forgotten. The message was not.

"He said, 'Coach ... I'm ready,'" Bennett said. "He said, 'That wasn't my best. I wasn't quite where I wanted to be or right in that ACC Tournament.'

"And he said, 'I desperately want to do anything — absolutely anything I can — to make this team advance. I know what last year was. This is what I'm so committed to.'"

Diakite needed to say it to make his coach believe in him, but also to make him believe in himself.

"I just threw a challenge to myself, in a sense, by telling him I got his back, we'll make it to the final and actually win it," Diakite said. "Telling him made me think about it every night, every day, every second I was working, and made me more hungry. I wanted to contribute for every game."

Diakite's experience with the historic upset from the year before differed from that of his teammates.

Growing up in Conakry, Guinea, a port town on the west coast of Africa's, Diakite didn't pay any attention whatsoever to college basketball. He knew nothing of the NCAA Tournament. He learned how to play by watching videos of Michael Jordan.

JON GOLDEN

Even when Diakite moved stateside at the start of high school to attend the Blue Ridge School in Virginia to hone his skills and search for Division I opportunities, he didn't pay much attention to the college landscape.

The first national championship game he watched was in 2016, at the conclusion of his first year on Grounds, which he had redshirted.

Two years later, when the Cavaliers lost to UMBC, he felt "ashamed." He was in for a surprise just hours later.

"I knew it was bad," Diakite said. "I didn't know how bad it was until we got on the bus, and we couldn't get in the hotel from the front. We had to go all the way back. And that's when I knew it was really bad."

Diakite has always been a player fueled by confidence. When equipped with the right mindset and preparation, he's a game-changer. So, when his confidence was shattered after the 2018 loss, it was Bennett who raised him back up, telling the team how good of a season it had, and how he was still proud of the players after the toughest of endings.

A year later, Diakite was determined to return the favor.

\*\*\*

Throughout the season, Diakite, who Bennett had deemed an "X-factor" at the beginning of the year, had shown great strides. He blocked shots and dunked lobs with authority. He defended without fouling, something that he had been unable to do his first two years.

He played with passion and intensity, sometimes allowing it to get the best of him, but usually with just the right amount. He would sky high for rebounds and snatch them down with two hands on the defensive end.

On the offensive end, if he couldn't get both hands there, he'd tip it out to a teammate, becoming one of college basketball's best and most valuable offensive rebounders.

He had always played hard. Now he was playing smart, too.

"His talent and his ability were important [heading into the season]," Bennett said. "And he has improved. He's newer to the game because of when he started playing. He's matured. He's had a really good season. … And I think that was the key to our success."

The numbers back that up. In his first two years, Diakite had never scored more than 12 points in a game. He surpassed that number six times in 2018-2019. He had a block in 20 straight games at one point. He had shown so much progress, which made his ACC Tournament failures so surprising. In past years, that stretch may have thrown him off-course.

This year, it proved to be a blessing in disguise. It refocused and re-energized Diakite. Things were never going to be easy. A March loss proved that. It might just have been the perfect reminder for the Cavaliers, too.

\*\*\*

"Last year" was happening again.

The 16th-seeded Gardner-Webb Runnin' Bulldogs led by as much as 14 and held a six-point advantage at halftime.

The Colonial Life Arena in Columbia, S.C., like the Spectrum Center just up Interstate 85 in Charlotte a year earlier, was loud, deafening, the partisans seeing the blood in the water.

Things were going all wrong for the Cavaliers.

But this wasn't Virginia of last year.

OK, for a while, an uncomfortable while, it felt like it.

Gardner-Webb actually led by 14 at two different points in the first half, hitting 15 of its first 24 shots from the floor in the process.

Then the Cavaliers turned the D on, holding the Bulldogs to a pair of threes in the final 6:52, as they cut into the margin to 36-30 at the halftime break.

The locker room at the half: strangely, calm.

"I remember last year, halftime against UMBC," Ty Jerome would say

SCOTT RATCLIFFE

postgame, "one of our coaches came in screaming at us, and we …".

"I was out there doing an interview. So, it wasn't me," Bennett said.

"We felt their panic last year at halftime, and that was one thing I remember, not doing a good job keeping everyone calm," Jerome continued. "That's what I pride myself on, too. Every timeout, it's just a matter of keeping guys calm, keeping guys calm, but also keeping our edge. You've got to find a balance. You can't come out, everything's going to be OK, stay calm. Just trying to find the right balance of staying calm and keeping our edge."

The calm, yet edgy, Cavaliers opened on a 14-2 run in the first 5:39 of the second half, taking their first lead of the game on a De'Andre Hunter and-one with 16:16 to go.

Then, after a David Efianayi three, UVA went on an 11-0 run, capped by a Braxton Key three-pointer with 10:17 left that pushed the Cavaliers' lead to 55-41.

The lead would remain in double-digits the rest of the way from there as Virginia posted a 71-56 win.

Phew!

The key, in addition to the calm edge, was defense: Gardner-Webb, after the hot start shooting, was just 7-of-22 (31.8 percent) from the floor in the second half, with 12 turnovers.

The Pack-Line did what it needed to do to shut down the Runnin' Bulldogs' forays into the lane. Gardner-Webb had been shooting 10-of-13 in the paint in the first 13-plus minutes. They would finish 12-of-22 in the paint, so, they were 2-of-9 in the final 27.

The solid effort on D, in turn, fueled the Virginia offense. UVA actually shot 50 percent from the floor in the first half, but eight first-half turnovers limited opportunities on the offensive end.

Diakite, for his part, dominated the Runnin' Bulldogs to the tune of 17 points (one short of his career high) and nine rebounds (a career high), in addition to his work helping seal down the paint.

There was clearly a concerted effort to get the ball inside to Diakite and Hunter (a combined 23 points, on 9-of-16 shooting, in the second half).

The comeback was also the result of heavy lifting done by the smallest guy on the roster, 5-foot-9 freshman guard Kihei Clark, whose counting numbers wouldn't impress anybody: three points, five rebounds, four assists in 36 minutes.

It was his defense – and, well, everything – that would be the difference.

Gardner-Webb tried multiple times in the second half to run a pick-and-roll with Jaheam Cornwall and Jose Perez, aimed at getting Clark, at 5-foot-9, one-one-one with Perez, at 6-foot-5, on the switch.

Perez wouldn't score on any of those sets, as Clark held his own: forcing Perez to pass, once stripping him of the ball, then bodying him up on a missed jumper.

His hands were everywhere: in passing lanes, picking up loose balls.

Virginia actually didn't lead in the game until Clark tracked down a 50/50 ball and found Hunter for a hoop-and-a-harm that made it 39-38 'Hoos with 16:16 to go.

For some reason, the official scorer didn't see fit to award Clark an assist there, but he did register one at the 14:21 mark on another pass to Hunter, who knocked down a short jumper that pushed the lead to 44-38.

He picked up three more assists – to Jerome for a three, and another two to Hunter, for a jumper and a three.

\*\*\*

The scene in the locker room postgame was unlike one you would ever see in the wake of a No. 1 seed just having put to bed a win over a No. 16.

The celebratory mood was well-earned.

"That will always be part of our story. I understand that," Bennett said. "I'm sure a lot of people thought it was going to be part of our story the second year in a row. But it's just now, this is a new year. This is trying to be in the moment, and that's a challenge to the best of your ability. So, now you get your rest, you prepare for Oklahoma, and get ready."

Oklahoma had done a lot of improving since the Sooners and Cavaliers had been together in the Bahamas for the Battle 4 Atlantis.

OU had lost to Wisconsin in the semifinals, so the two teams hadn't met back in November.

A five-game losing streak, spanning from Jan. 28 to Feb. 11, had put Oklahoma on the NCAA Tournament bubble, and a one-and-done appearance in the Big 12 Tournament, and a 72-71 loss to West Virginia that sent the Sooners packing early, had some wondering if they'd get an invite to the Big Dance.

Not only did they, but they were a nine seed, and then the Sooners lit up Ole Miss in their first-round game, getting out to an early 12-0 lead and coasting to a 95-72 win.

They had 50 at halftime in the first round. They wouldn't get to 51 in the Round of 32 until there was 1:35 left to go in the game.

It was a gloriously boring Virginia win.

A Key three with 3:45 to go in the first half put Virginia up 10, and the lead would remain in double-digits for all but 63 seconds the rest of the way.

No 7-foot-6 guys dunking on their tiptoes, no Zion Williamson dunks, no stickbacks off missed free throws to take the lead, as fans in the Colonial Life Arena had just taken in earlier in the afternoon, in the Duke-Central Florida game that would be the first of three straight games for the top overall tournament seed that would come down to the final play.

What you got out of Virginia's win was a lot of hard hedge, closeouts on threes, help on dives, ball screens, pocket passes.

Ruthless efficiency.

Boring basketball.

No drama.

Just the way Virginia fans like their basketball.

It was certainly a far cry from the scene in the first-round game two days earlier, which had seen Gardner-Webb light up the 'Hoos in the first half, in front of a highly partisan crowd – the school, two hours up the road, had to have closed down for the day, and relocated to Columbia.

The atmosphere on this Sunday night was cold after the Duke-UCF classic sucked all of the air out of the arena.

Emotionally spent, fans needed something on the court to get them back into their job of being ... fans.

Virginia, at its best, will starve any arena not named after John Paul Jones of its oxygen, with stifling defense and coolly efficient offense.

Both were at play in this one.

Oklahoma had an early 13-2 spurt to take a brief four-point first-half lead, but an 18-2 UVA response, over a 9:41 stretch, gave the 'Hoos a 12-point lead, and the way things were going at that stage, if you'd seen Virginia at all before, you had a good feeling where this one was going.

"They got us out of rhythm," said Brady Manek, a 6-foot-9 stretch four, who had 13 points in the first half, on 5-of-9 shooting, but didn't score a point in the second half, missing all four of his shots from the field, as Bennett sicced Hunter and Key on him in the final 20 minutes.

Oklahoma shot 36.5 percent for the night, just 6-of-13 on shots in the paint.

Against Ole Miss, OU shot 57.6 percent, and was 22-of-32 in the paint.

"Just trying to get in the pack and make it more difficult for them to get inside," Key explained the defensive focus to reporters afterward. "When they got inside, just post trapping their guards, and try to give them different looks that they may not have seen prior to today."

But, see, that's boring.

Nothing there about poster dunks, highlight-reel blocked shots.

It was cold, impersonal, business-like.

And a thing of absolute beauty, if you're a Virginia fan.

\*\*\*

There was more to the X's and O's than the move to shut down Manek in the second half.

Bennett went with Diakite in the post over Salt to match up with Oklahoma forward Kristian Doolittle, who averaged 11.3 points and 7.1 rebounds a game in 2018-2019, but was maybe a bit of a liability on the defensive end, at least with what Bennett and the coaching staff had in mind with Diakite.

"[Diakite] started the second half against Gardner-Webb, and we thought, well, Jack Salt is so physical, and we thought maybe he could play one-on-one against [Doolittle]," Bennett explained afterwards. "But what we wanted to do offensively, I thought there was some more scoring opportunities for how we were going to attack for Mamadi, how to roll and get on the rim and make some plays.

"And then [Diakite's] quickness, I thought, might be a factor."

The move paid off, as Diakite led the team in scoring (14 points on 7-of-9 shooting), rebounding (Diakite and Key each hauled down nine) and blocked shots (three of them, all in the first half).

"I wasn't trying to force anything. ... I was locked in, and I was trying to respond to the challenge [Coach Bennett] gave me. He started me tonight, and I wanted to prove to him that I was ready to play, so, I did so," Diakite said after the game.

Bennett explained that he was contemplating the decision to start Diakite Sunday morning, and Diakite said that Bennett pulled him aside and let him know that he had a "responsibility to help the team, and we're trusting you," as Diakite recalled.

"He's matured," added Bennett. "I think a key is, he allowed us to play

Doolittle one-on-one in the post. Mamadi's quickness off the floor [could] bother maybe his mid-range shot and just work so we didn't have to come and trap."

\*\*\*

Bennett can do the X's and O's. He also knows how to slip into Dr. Phil mode when needed.

"Only the guys in the locker room and the coaching staff who were part of last year's team and this year's team can truly appreciate and understand," Bennett said after the game, stopping his thought about last year's misery and this year's revival.

"We tried to get back to this spot, even to be a [No.] 1 seed, and then to have to go into the situation and to be down in [the Gardner-Webb] game, definitely pressure in terms of the game. That was real. You could feel it. And to show the resilience to kind of get through that …"

Again, he didn't finish his thought. He didn't have to.

The whole basketball world was watching. Most of that world was cheering because of the way Bennett and his team handled last year's shock and awe with poise and dignity.

"Frankly, he didn't have to say much before tonight's game," Kyle Guy said afterward. "It's March, it's the Round of 32. None of us have ever been beyond that before except for Jack [Salt]. You don't need much [motivation]. Coach [Bennett] knew the monkey was off our back, he knew what we were thinking."

The proverbial monkey may have disappeared for most of the team, but not for Guy. There's a screensaver on his phone of him on his knees, weeping after last year's loss to UMBC, the No. 16 seed celebrating in the background.

It had been a daily reminder, a driving force behind Guy's determination to get back to this place.

"It's gone for some people," Guy said. "I'm never going to forget."

It wasn't the pressure of the moment that affected his shooting performance in eliminating the Sooners. He was 0-for-10 from behind the arc, and scored four points, but had five rebounds and three assists, including a crowd-pleasing, behind-the-back pass under the basket to Key.

"I think we only played our hardest for 30 or 32 minutes on Friday [against Gardner-Webb]," Guy said. "Tonight, we played for the full 40, and that's what it's going to take. It's going to be a battle of wills for the rest of the way. We played our asses off tonight."

Guy pointed out that if just the pressure of opening the tournament with the UMBC thing hanging over Virginia, the fact that Gardner-Webb made some tough shots the first half reminded the Cavaliers of last year when UMBC made everything it tossed up.

"We made some mistakes against Gardner-Webb, and we made some tonight, too, but Oklahoma didn't make as many shots as Gardner-Webb," Guy said.

It was now on to Louisville and the Sweet Sixteen for a late-night Thursday game against a 12th-seeded Oregon team that defeated UC-Irvine.

"Survive and advance," Guy smiled.

# CHAPTER 8
# Sweet, to Elite

Oregon was maybe the hottest team in the country, having had to play its way into the NCAA Tournament by winning four games in the Pac-12 Tourney.

The Ducks had won 10 in a row overall, their last loss coming more than a month earlier.

Most troubling for Virginia: Oregon was almost a carbon copy of the last team with a W over the 'Hoos, Florida State – big, long, athletic.

The Sweet Sixteen game started a lot like the FSU game in Charlotte, as the Ducks built a 16-10 lead midway through the first half, with UVA making just four of its first 20 shots from the floor.

Just like in each of the first two Big Dance victories, the Cavaliers used a 13-2 scoring run to take a five-point lead, and Mamadi Diakite made a nice move in the final seconds to give the Cavaliers a 30-22 halftime advantage.

The eight-point lead felt comfortable, but it wasn't over, not by a long shot.

The Ducks took their final lead of the night with 5:41 to go on a Louis King three-pointer that gave his team a 45-42 edge.

After King's go-ahead three (his third made three in a row), Kihei Clark answered right back with a triple of his own, his third — and biggest — of the night, to tie it back up.

De'Andre Hunter came away with a steal on the ensuing trip before Ty Jerome delivered another huge three-ball with 3:33 left on the clock, giving the 'Hoos a 48-45 lead, and they would not relinquish it.

The score would stay right there, though, and uncomfortably so, for Virginia fans, until Kyle Guy found Hunter mysteriously wide open in the paint for the dagger, an easy lay-in that pushed the Cavalier lead to five with just 27 ticks showing.

The Wahoos' offensive numbers may not have been the greatest — 36 percent from the field (20-for-56) and just 27 percent (9-for-33) from deep — but as Jerome described, Tony Bennett's message during a timeout with 4:42 to go was very clear.

"[Coach Bennett] called a set for us to run, and he said, 'But, what matters is our defense,'" Jerome recalled. "That's what carried us all year, and that's what's going to take us as far as we can, as far as we want to go."

Diakite grabbed a career-high 11 rebounds in a low-scoring game in which every possession was vital.

Less than two weeks prior, he had shriveled against a similarly athletic and imposing Florida State team. Now he was shining when his team needed him most.

"I thought Mamadi's rebounding was significant in that game," Bennett said. "We needed that."

\*\*\*

And now, Virginia was on the verge of a berth in the Final Four, a first for Bennett, and a first for the program since way back in 1984.

It was so close that everyone could taste it.

Though, caution, we'd been there before.

Bennett's 2015-2016 team, definitely a Final Four-worthy squad, should have made it to Houston that March, before Syracuse happened. UVA blew a big lead, and the Orange, a team that many had argued didn't belong in the tournament, staged an incredible rally to steal a Final Four trip from the Cavaliers' grasp.

Now, Virginia was awaiting a tipoff against Purdue — another program that hadn't been to the Final Four since the 1980s — in the NCAA South Regional finals.

The winner earned a trip to Minneapolis, site of the 2019 Final Four.

Bennett actually had been part of a Final Four team, his father Dick Bennett's team, at Wisconsin in 2000.

Tony Bennett had finished his NBA career, and knew his father was edging toward retirement. He just wanted to be his side and enjoy the ride.

"Bang, that first year I'm a volunteer manager, and [his father] goes to the Final Four," Tony said. "I'm like, 'That seems pretty easy and pretty fun. Maybe I'll get into this coaching thing.' I didn't realize how tough it was."

Hanging over his head going into this one was the idea that the 2018-2019 season wouldn't be a success in the minds of many unless Virginia made it to the Final Four.

Bennett also had some personal skin in the game. One of the game's best coaches, there were detractors – loud detractors – saying he couldn't be considered among the elite until he got his team to the sport's biggest stage.

"I'd love if it happened, but if it doesn't happen, you have to say, 'Hey, are you going to be OK?' And that's what I learned, and that's invaluable. So, I'm at peace, but I'm very hungry," Bennett said on the eve of the game.

Losing to UMBC last season had changed Bennett, in a way, he conceded.

"It created a fire in me that made me want to become a better coach and pursue trying to get these guys to as far as they can, a Final Four, a national championship," Bennett said. "It's burning hot, but it did something I think maybe as significant or greater. It made me realize that if that never does happen, I'll still be OK, because I've been blessed beyond what I deserve.

"I think that has freed me up to go after this as hard as I can, as hard as we can," Bennett added. "Do these guys want this? Does Purdue want this? Do I want that? Would I love to be a son and father who coached in a Final Four? That would be great."

\*\*\*

Would Carsen Edwards ever miss?

Purdue as a team seemed to be in the zone, hitting four of its first five shots, three of them threes, on the way to building an early 22-12 lead.

It seemed that the Boilermakers were set to run Virginia out of the gym, and the partisan crowd – roughly 75 percent Purdue fans, and they were loud – were eating up every minute of it.

Virginia went on a 12-3 run over the following five minutes of play — highlighted by a pair of Jerome three-pointers — to cut the deficit to one, 25-24, with 4:46 left until the break.

Diakite had a big first half, and finished it off with a bucket off a nice feed from Clark (who hustled to get his own rebound and set up the shot) with a minute to go, and the 'Hoos went into the locker room down 30-29.

There was a scary moment just before halftime. Guy stepped on a foot trying to fight through a screen, and went to the floor, screaming in pain.

He said later that he heard a pop, which, anybody who has ever played pickup basketball knows, sprain.

To that point he was shooting 1-for-6 from the floor for the night, and 9-of-44 in the 2019 NCAA Tournament.

The MVPs for the 'Hoos may be the members of the training staff who fixed Guy up and got him back out there. Guy made his first four three-point attempts of the second half on his way to putting up 19 second-half points on 7-of-12 shooting.

Guy would finish with 25 points and 10 rebounds.

Jerome had 24 points and seven assists for the Cavaliers.

Those numbers suggest what you'd think they'd suggest: that Virginia put some numbers on the board in the second half.

So did Purdue. Edwards had a brief lull toward the end of the first half, and then Bennett came back with what you'd assume was the ultimate equalizer, in the form of Hunter, the ACC Defensive Player of the Year.

The 6-foot-1 Edwards was getting first-half looks over the 5-foot-9 Clark, so, good luck, getting looks over the 6-foot-7 Hunter.

Edwards' response: to step back out to 25 feet, 30 feet, 35 feet, on one connection.

The junior finished with 42 points, sinking 10 threes, and the second half was a back-and-forth-and-back-again as the teams traded buckets.

Edwards seemed to have made the biggest shot of the night, banking in a three with 1:10 to go to put Purdue up 69-67.

Bennett, on the sideline, after the bank, which reminded Virginia fans, ominously, of the banked three by Hunter that had beaten Louisville in this building a year earlier, ripped his play card in half.

"Just ripped it in half," Bennett would say afterward.

Guy missed from three with 46 seconds to go, and Purdue had the chance to put the game away, but Edwards missed a three-pointer with 22 seconds left.

Grady Eifert corralled the miss, and got the ball to Ryan Cline, who was fouled with 16 seconds to go.

Cline, a 71-percent foul shooter on the season, missed the back end of the one-and-one, leaving the door open for Virginia.

Purdue coach Matt Painter played strategy, having his team foul Jerome before he could get off a potential game-tying three.

Jerome made the front end with 5.9 seconds left, and then appeared to miss the second intentionally, though he would say after the game that, no, not intentional.

More on that later.

And anyway, the effect was the same.

\*\*\*

Diakite got his hands on the rebound, tipping it back.

Remember Craig Robinson, tipping a missed free throw back to Ralph Sampson, in Ralph's last home game at University Hall?

That one was smooth. Ralph got that one at the free-throw line.

Actually, this one went back to the free-throw line, too, just, on the Purdue side of the court.

Clark, water bug that he is, tracked it down with 3.2 seconds to go.

That's what we had left in UVA's season of redemption at that stage.

The 'Hoos had a timeout in their pocket, but this is a scramble play. You're not thinking timeouts in this kind of situation.

What's going through Clark's mind as he turns back upcourt?

"I knew we didn't have much time," Clark said.

His options: he could have tried a half-court heave.

Or passed the ball to Jerome, to his right, at half-court.

Or to Guy, who was at half-court on the left side.

Purdue had scrambled down the floor chasing the ball as well, and inexplicably seemed focused on preventing one of the three half-court options.

Again, this is what happens in scramble situations.

This all leaves Jack Salt, standing at the three-point line on the left wing, and Diakite, just right of the lane, and only Matt Haarms back to defend both.

It happens that Haarms is 7-foot-3. This almost factors in.

Getting ahead of ourselves there.

Clark, pretty much on Pluto, back in the backcourt, saw Diakite "right away," and rifled the ball to him, the ball leaving his hands near midcourt with 2.0 seconds left.

What was going through Diakite's mind?

"I don't know. It happened," said Diakite, who caught the pass with right at 1.0 seconds left, about 10 feet from the basket, and released it almost immediately, in the direction of the rim, replays showing it out of his hands, and just over the outstretched arms of Haarms, with two-tenths of a second on the clock.

Splash.

Bedlam.

Overtime.

Divine intervention, if you ask Diakite.

"I was the person who was designed to take it. And I don't know. I took it, and it went in," said Diakite, not normally at a loss for words, who found himself, not surprisingly, given the magnitude of the moment, tongue-tied.

"I don't know how to talk about it. It was unbelievable. I don't know how to talk about it. I don't know," Diakite said.

It happened so perfectly that it did indeed seemed to have been some part of design, as Diakite alluded.

It wasn't.

Jerome insisted later that he didn't intentionally miss the second free throw.

"I made the first on purpose," said Jerome, to laughter in the media room.

Jerome also happened to be at the line at the end of a game a year ago in the very KFC Yum! Center where this one for the ages took place, at the scene of another amazing Virginia comeback, from four down with nine-tenths of a second left.

Jerome made the first two of a three-shot foul in that one, against Louisville, then missed the third intentionally, before a lane violation on

Virginia, an inbound violation by Louisville, and a buzzer-beating Hunter three, sent Virginia home the improbable winner.

Jerome said he just short-armed this one, intending to make the shot to get his team back to within one.

"Mamadi did a good play by hitting it, and Kihei made the play of the century, and Mamadi being ready to shoot. Actually, let me add, he looked me off first, or looked Kyle off first, and then looked me off. Then he got to Mamadi over here, and he made a great play," Jerome said.

Jerome, you can see on the replay, is trying to get Clark's attention to get the ball for a last desperation heave.

Bennett was thinking, from the sideline, yeah, that.

"Ty was clapping. I was like, 'Throw it to Ty. We'll get one up there,'" Bennett said. "Mamadi, to catch it and get it off that quick, so improbable.

"Two years ago, what happened here, we've had amazing games here and comebacks. I was almost in shock a little bit."

*Was?* How about, *still am?*

\*\*\*

There was still a game to win.

Haarms put the Boilermakers ahead early in the overtime, but Jerome came down and floated one in high off the glass, out of Haarms' reach.

Nojel Easter split a pair of free throws on one end. Then Hunter sank a pair on the other to give UVA a 74-73 edge with 1:43 left.

Edwards' (and Purdue's) final basket came with 42 ticks showing, putting the Boilermakers back up by one. Hunter responded with a drive to the hole to put the 'Hoos up to stay with 26 seconds left.

Edwards misfired on a stepback three-pointer on the ensuing trip, and Guy was fouled on the rebound with 5.7 seconds to go, and added a pair of free throws to make it a three-point game.

Purdue turned the ball over as an Edwards pass was tipped and deflected off of one of his teammates, and the possession was awarded to the Cavaliers.

After a video review, 2.1 seconds were put on the clock, and Clark put the icing on the Final Four cake with two sealing free throws, as the 'Hoos began to celebrate.

They were Final Four-bound.

\*\*\*

When the clock struck zero and sent all of Virginia into a Final Fourgasm, Guy, in all the euphoria, flashed back to a darker time last March.

We all remember the scenario. Guy was emotionally crushed, having dropped to his knees in anguish, tears rushing down his reddened face while the Cinderella of all Cinderellas, UMBC, celebrated the NCAA Tournament's first No. 16 seed upset over a No. 1.

Guy never forgot that moment, that heartbreak. He'll never forget. For the past year, that haunting photograph has served as a daily reminder as a screensaver on his phone. It served as a daily fire in his belly to get back to the madness of March.

His nightmare had finally come to an end.

Guy finished with a team-high 25 points, shooting 7-of-13 from the field the second half and overtime, including 5-of-9 from beyond the arc.

When it was over, Guy unashamedly experienced that flashback and dismissed it to the scrap heap of his memory.

"Flashing back to when I was on my knees last year, and you know, just overflowing with joy," said Guy, sporting a championship hat and shirt emblazoned with "A Cut Above" slogan passed out by the NCAA.

"So happy for my teammates and my coaches and for myself to be able to break through in the way that we did this year," Guy smiled a toothy grin. "Not only did we silence [Bennett's] critics, we silenced our own."

While the rest of Wahoo Nation was wondering what was wrong with Guy during his extended slump, and the Purdue fans were all over him for a lack of production in the first half, the former "Mr. Basketball" in Indiana never sweated.

Well, if he did, he didn't let the rest of us see it.

"I told you guys, I don't really believe in slumps, and I always found rhythm when my guys are trying to find me," Guy said. "Ty [Jerome], Kihei [Clark], Dre [De'Andre Hunter], they were all looking for me, even though I struggled in the past few games. All the credit goes to them."

There were huge moments for each of the Cavaliers in this drama-packed regional final.

Jerome's big shots, keeping UVA alive. Hunter's work inside the circle, Salt's work on the boards and on defense, Clark's best-defense-possible on Edwards and offensive floor work, and another incredible NCAA performance by Diakite.

But the night belonged to Guy with his dramatic second-half comeback, the onslaught of points, not to mention a team-high 10 rebounds.

No more tears, no more shame. Only exhilaration.

He's gonna need a new screensaver.

\*\*\*

On March 30, 2009 — 10 years to the day of Virginia's Elite Eight win — Virginia hired Tony Bennett.

He brought a system that would take time: not only time on the shot clock, but time, as in years, to build the Cavaliers into a contender.

There were rough patches. Virginia won 31 games in his first two seasons at the helm combined.

(For reference, the team would win 35 times in 2018-2019.)

Bennett's first trip to the NCAA Tournament ended in a 26-point first round loss, and the program was in the NIT the next year.

Since then, Virginia has gone to six consecutive NCAA Tournaments, the longest such streak in school history.

There's been hope and heartbreak, exuberance and embarrassment, triumph and tears.

Tears, especially, after last year.

You wonder why Bennett let out that roar as he descended the ladder after having made the last snip on the net in the KFC Yum! Center?

He'd tried to lighten the mood with his team in the locker room after the Gardner-Webb win in the first round by walking in with a stuffed monkey on his back that he then dramatically threw down to signify, yes, it was silly, but, the monkey was off their backs.

It was emphatic now.

Virginia, Tony Bennett, would now be in the Final Four.

Finally.

Perhaps now the critics who said UVA couldn't win in March, that Bennett Ball was ruining the college game, that Bennett couldn't get a team to the Big Dance, would finally get off his back.

# CHAPTER 9
# Three free throws

The lights were brighter, the stage much bigger, and the setting unlike one Virginia had been to since 1984.

One week after the Cavaliers had defeated Purdue in overtime, the Final Four stage was set for them to face Auburn in Minneapolis.

All week, the Cavaliers had downplayed worries about shooting in a football stadium rather than a normal basketball arena, pointing to their 18-for-25 three-point performance at Syracuse's Carrier Dome, which houses both sports. They had dismissed worries about the bright lights being too much to handle; this was a veteran-laden team, after all.

CRYSTAL GRAHAM

While they hadn't been on this stage before, they had been under the microscope all season for how they would respond to last year's season-ending loss. They handled interviews with aplomb. They smiled and laughed during their open practice at U.S. Bank Stadium.

They were, for all intents and purposes, as ready and as loose as they'd ever be.

"We try to do it with a smile on our face," Kyle Guy said. "We've been through so much and have been doubted pretty much all of Coach Bennett's tenure here."

That attitude showed early, as the Cavaliers used a series of backscreens and backdoor cuts to take advantage of the Tigers' hyper-aggressive man-to-man scheme. Against one of the best and most hellacious units in college basketball, Virginia turned it over just three times in the opening 20 minutes.

But Auburn, too, was operating at a high level, using its speedy guards to get to the rim. With the Tigers leading 26-25 late in the first half, Jared Harper took it coast-to-coast to lay it in, incensing Tony Bennett on the sideline. The normally calm head coach turned his head in disgust and had some words for his players as they came up the court the ensuing possession.

The Tigers, normally a perimeter-scoring team, led 31-28 at halftime on the strength of 18 points in the paint.

That didn't sit well with the man whose defense was built to limit just that.

"I thought we had some errors defensively," Bennett said. "One, we weren't

back the way we needed to against them … and then we let the ball get in the lane too much. We weren't [doing] what we thought we needed to do. … They were getting downhill, touching the paint, and that put too much pressure. They're so quick. And they went by us, and we needed to collectively, we always say, build a wall or impact when we could."

Another issue was the continued struggles of De'Andre Hunter on the offensive end. One of the Cavaliers' top scorers, Hunter had been held in check in games against Oklahoma, Oregon and Purdue, and against Auburn, he was struggling again.

The only player on either team who played the entire first half, Hunter had shot just 2-of-6 from the field: a layup and an open mid-range jumper after two Auburn defenders had collided. The talented wing scorer had looked pensive at times, and his team needed him to get going.

On the very first play of the second half, Hunter set a screen for Guy, who came curling off it. Guy has thrived on that motion and buried three-pointers off of it his entire career in Virginia; he had done so early in the first half of this very game, in fact.

This time, when Guy caught the ball, both Malik Dunbar, his primary defender, and Danjel Purifoy, Hunter's defender, stepped toward the Cavaliers' shooting guard.

Guy then dumped it off, and Hunter took one power dribble before finishing at the rim.

On the very next offensive possession, Hunter caught a pass on the wing, immediately attacked toward the basket and rattled home a one-handed fadeaway.

Just like that, Virginia had regained the lead, and its leading scorer had regained some confidence.

On the other end, Hunter delivered a massive block on Bryce Brown's dunk attempt, and Virginia used an 8-0 run out of halftime to build a 36-31 lead.

The game remained tight, with Auburn answering every time Virginia threatened to pull away. The largest the Cavaliers' lead grew was seven with just under nine minutes to go, but Auburn responded with the next four consecutive points to make it 50-47.

Throughout the season, Virginia had a devastating run, the Cavalanche, usually in the second half, to put away opponent after opponent. The Tigers were determined to not become the next victim.

But then, Virginia embarked on that run again. It started with Ty Jerome, whose off-balance floater from the elbow somehow found the bottom of the net, extending the lead to five. Then Hunter muscled through the Auburn defense for a tough layup.

Then came a staple of the Virginia playbook. Guy dribbled to the corner, reverse pivoted and fired a pass to the wing to Jerome, who had been freed by a Mamadi Diakite screen. The three-pointer was the rightful culmination to a play run to perfection.

Guy pumped both fists. The Cavaliers bench burst with excitement. Auburn coach Bruce Pearl needed a timeout. The Cavalier faithful occupying the northwest corner of the stadium shrieked in excitement.

This was the Cavalanche that was sending Virginia — now up 57-47 with just over five minutes to play — to the championship.

They had ground the speedy Auburn attack to a halt and displayed brutal efficiency on offense. At that point, the Cavaliers owned a 28-15 advantage in the second half.

"I thought we got enough cushion," Kihei Clark said.

\*\*\*

The Auburn Tigers were never one to quit. When they lost three games in a row to fall out of the Top 25, they responded with three straight double-digit wins. When they took a 27-point loss on the chin at Kentucky, they responded with four straight wins to end the regular season and another four to capture the SEC Tournament championship. When they lost star forward Chuma Okeke late in their Sweet Sixteen game against North Carolina, they not only vanquished the Tar Heels, but then defeated Kentucky in the Elite Eight two days later.

Auburn was made up of underdogs. Brown and Anfernee McLemore were low-rated recruits. For Harper, the team's 5-foot-11 heart and soul, Auburn was his only high-major offer. The Tigers never let the odds define them. A 10-point deficit, even against Virginia, wasn't going to discourage them in the least.

"I feel like we've been in the underdog role a lot," Harper had said. "I've been in the underdog role my entire life. We're taking it as it comes. We know what we can do. We know that at the end of the day, it matters what we believe in and what we feel like we can do."

They started chipping away, and they got a major self-inflicted wound by the Cavaliers to help their cause.

After Samir Doughty made a free throw to cut it to single digits, Jerome missed a turnaround jumper after a hit across the arm from Harper went uncalled. A frustrated Jerome made a beeline for Harper and hacked him, his fourth foul.

He was forced to the sideline after what he later called a "bonehead" play.

Bennett could hardly believe his pupil had let his emotions get the best of him.

"Why did you do that?" the exasperated coach asked Jerome on his way to the bench.

The Tigers took full advantage. Brown nailed a three to cut it to six. The triple was his 139th of the season, breaking the single-season SEC record. And he wasn't done. A corner three the next trip down the court cut the deficit to three.

A putback from Purifoy cut it to one, and another corner three from Brown, off an ingenious fade cut, gave the Tigers their first lead since early in the second half at 59-57 with 1:56 left.

"All season long, we've been through a lot of adversity, and coach does a good job of just keeping us together," Brown said. "I feel like, at the end of the day in the game, we stayed together. That's why we were able to make that run."

Now it was the Tigers who had their offense rolling, and the Cavaliers who had ground to a halt. Without Jerome, the Cavaliers were lost, and even when he returned, he struggled to find his earlier form. He missed back-to-back threes, and Virginia's chances grew slimmer.

With 17 seconds left, McLemore buried a pair of free throws to make the Auburn lead four, 61-57. It was a 14-0 run. The Cavaliers had gone over five minutes without scoring.

Bennett called for a quick screen to free Guy, and, despite near-perfect defense from Doughty, Guy nailed the corner trifecta.

The clock showed 6.5 seconds when Clark fouled Harper, an 83.1-percent free throw shooter on the season, but the officials reviewed the clock at the scorer's table and added nine-tenths of a second back, which would prove crucial later.

Harper, after the wait, nailed the first free throw, but missed the second, and Virginia still had life.

Jerome pulled in the rebound and turned to speed up the court, but was quickly, purposely, fouled by Doughty. It was only Auburn's fifth team foul. They could still foul again to give Virginia even less time to find a shot, still one more foul away from the bonus.

On the ensuing inbound, Jerome initially lost the ball, but regathered it, and was fouled by Brown. In real time, it was hard to tell that Jerome had indeed gotten away with a double-dribble, as replay confirmed. But it also looked as if Brown had tugged Jerome's jersey as well.

Both infractions went uncalled, and Brown's foul came with 1.5 seconds left and Virginia near midcourt.

The Tigers had still executed their plan well: give the Cavaliers as little time as possible to find a reasonable shot. Bennett called for timeout.

The resulting play gave the Cavaliers what they needed. A three-man stack of Guy, Diakite and Hunter saw Diakite curl off toward the rim for a potential lob, and Guy come off a Hunter screen and dart to the near corner. Jerome delivered a perfect pass, and Guy turned, jumped aimed and fired.

Short. The Cavaliers had lost.

Foul. The Cavaliers were still alive.

The PA announcer boomed that Auburn had won, but the reactions of the players told a different story.

Guy knowingly nodded his head and collected high-fives from his teammates. Auburn center Austin Wiley put his hands on his head in disbelief and walked in the opposite direction.

On the Virginia bench, Kody Stattmann's jaw dropped. "I thought they weren't gonna call it," he said.

But referee James Breeding had indeed called a foul on Doughty, who had undercut Guy.

The clock was set to show six-tenths of a second remaining.

Remember the nine-tenths that had been added back after the Guy three? Without that, it is game over.

Instead, it was Guy, the poster boy for the failure of last March, headed to the free-throw line for three shots down two points.

Welcome to your moment, Kyle Guy.

\*\*\*

"Calm is contagious."

That was the message the Cavaliers preached throughout the season. When the Cavaliers went to overtime at N.C. State and had to close out a game with two starters fouled out and another one ailing, calm was contagious. When they came back from a late-second half deficit to secure a key road win at North Carolina, calm was contagious.

When they overcame a raucous crowd at Virginia Tech for the first sweep of the Hokies since 2015, calm was contagious. When they rallied past Louisville, calm was contagious. In the first round of the ACC Tournament, when they turned a slow start against N.C. State into a 20-point win, calm was contagious.

When they dispatched Gardner-Webb after another poor first half and again won the following week with an overtime thriller over Purdue, calm was contagious.

Being calm in high-leverage situations in regular-season games is one thing. Being calm there, and then, in front of 71,000 people screaming, booing, watching, waiting and chomping fingernails into stubs, was another.

Guy wasn't catching the calmness. He retreated away from that boisterous crowd, away from the game, away from even his own teammates, and inside his own jersey.

He covered his face. He tried to find that calmness. It didn't work.

"I could lie to you and say I knew I was going to hit them, but I was terrified," he'd go on to tell CBS.

Terrified or not, he had a job to do. And those few moments inside his own jersey may have saved him.

"I didn't want to have anything to do with my teammates or coaches at that time," Guy explained. "I just wanted to be in my own space. I knew they had confidence in me. I just needed to build up my own. And we all practiced those shots as a kid."

He made the first — arguably the most important, because if he had missed, even two straight makes after that would only send it to overtime.

He made the second, and Pearl called timeout — Virginia would do no worse than force the extra session.

Scratch that. Virginia would win the game, right there, right then, with Guy at the line.

"It wasn't even, 'If he misses, or, if he makes it,'" walk-on Austin Katstra said. "It was, 'When he makes it, this is how we're gonna line up so they can't get a full-court heave.' We all have confidence in him. We all knew he was going to make it."

He made the third. Auburn's wild attempt at the buzzer went awry. After going five minutes and 15 seconds without scoring a point, the Cavaliers scored six points in the final 7.4 seconds. And while debate would rage about calls missed and calls made, Pearl, even on the losing end of things, would have none of it.

"Don't let [the foul] define the game, because then you're taking away from Ty Jerome, or you're taking away from Anfernee McLemore with 12 rebounds, or Bryce Brown almost leading Auburn back to an incredible come-from-behind victory. I'd love that to be the story," Pearl said.

Pearl was spot-on when he called out Jerome. Though Guy played hero, it was Jerome who played the most complete game there was that night. He had 21 points and six assists, both game highs, and collected nine rebounds, a team high. Against one of the best turnover-forcing teams in the nation, Jerome had just two giveaways.

"He played freakin' phenomenal," Guy said. "He carried us through this game."

SCOTT RATCLIFFE

It was clear that Jerome's play was absolutely essential to the Cavaliers' success. He posted a plus-minus of plus-6, the best on the Cavaliers by a three-point margin. Auburn's biggest run came when he was strapped to the bench.

"Luckily, we somehow came out on top, so I get another chance to play Monday," Jerome said. "But to put myself on the bench and leave my teammates like that in crunch time is a terrible decision."

In the aftermath, the Cavaliers' locker room celebration was subdued. Jerome attributed it to the team being so close to its ultimate goal.

Perhaps it was that, or that they still were processing how the previous few minutes had played out. That was Guy's theory.

"To be able to go to the national championship off of that for these guys and Coach Bennett, I really don't have the words," he said.

\*\*\*

Time for some accounting.

Guy scored six points in 7.4 seconds, including the three pressure-packed free throws with sixth-tenths of a second remaining, to help Virginia defeat Auburn.

That drama followed the miracle win over Purdue in the Elite Eight, when Mamadi Diakite etched his name into the annals of UVA basketball history.

How many times had we seen Virginia claw its way back from adversity this season, beating the odds with an improbable play? Even a year ago, who could ever forget the miraculous comeback at Louisville when the Cavaliers scored five points in nine-tenths of a second to pull off a stunning win?

It started to remind fans of another team that continued to defy probability, Jim Valvano's 1983 "Team of Destiny" at N.C. State.

Certainly, there are significant differences. That Wolfpack team didn't smell a No. 1 seed for its body of work. It was 20-10 entering the NCAA Tournament, and only finished 8-6 in the ACC.

No one believed that State would last long in the NCAA Tournament, let alone go on a magical six-game winning streak and win the whole thing, stunning No. 1 seed Virginia and Ralph Sampson in order to get to Albuquerque and the Final Four, then knocking off Houston's Phi Slama Jama in a championship game that we'll all remember.

"When you're on a roll, who knows what can happen," the late Jimmy V said about that ride. "The key for us is to be down five with 30 seconds left. That's when we start doing our best."

Valvano's quote may sound familiar to Wahoo fans, who had watched their team pull off some unbelievable wins.

In the '83 roll that Valvano mentioned, in the Wolfpack's opening game, it trailed Pepperdine by six with 24 seconds remaining in overtime. State won in double overtime, 69-67.

Then the 'Pack upset No. 3 seed UNLV, 71-70, on a last-second tip-in by Thurl Bailey. State went on to beat Utah, 75-56, then stunned Sampson-led Virginia, regarded as the best team in the nation, 63-62, to reach the Final Four.

In Albuquerque, State downed Georgia, 67-60, setting up what appeared to be a mismatch with highly-talented Houston.

Who will ever forget the buzzer-beating dunk by Lorenzo Charles when Derek Whittenburg's 30-foot jump shot came up short, sending Jimmy V into a frantic dance all over the floor, looking for someone to embrace?

State's Cinderella run was so amazing that ESPN made a "30 for 30" documentary of the whole thing, entitled "Survive and Advance."

That's what it's all about.

There have been plenty of hugs and celebrations along the way, at Louisville's KFC Yum! Center following Virginia's win over Purdue, then again on this particular Saturday night in cavernous U.S. Bank Stadium, at the Final Four, when Guy was mauled by his teammates in minutes of jubilation.

Guy blew kisses to UVA fans as he exited the court to a chorus of boos by Auburn fans who didn't agree with the foul call that sent him to the line for the game-winning free throws.

When the Wahoos got back to their locker room after the national semifinal win, Bennett had one strong piece of advice to his team: "We're not done yet."

During the interviews on the eve of the title game, the question had to be asked: is Virginia a "Team of Destiny?"

"I believe our steps are ordered," said Bennett, a man of strong faith, during Sunday's Final Four interview session. "I think you walk and you do everything you can with the abilities you've been given as players, as coaches, and then you trust.

"I just, I believe that. So, the fact that we're here, yeah, I think there's been a hand in this. In my life, I'd be foolish not to believe that."

Virginia's players and coaches believed they wouldn't be there, playing for a national championship on the Monday night in April that had been the goal all season long, had it not been for the stunning loss to No. 16 seed UMBC in last year's first round.

Guy said that doubt never creeped in, that "we're going to find a way to win ... just stay disciplined. We make so many adjustments, coaching adjustments, player adjustments, we do what it takes to win."

Maybe the Cavaliers' run hasn't been quite as dramatic as N.C. State's was in '83, although a couple of the UVA wins have perhaps been even more dramatic.

State's was more improbable unless you inject last year's Virginia nightmare into the equation, leaving the majority of the sporting public holding fast to a belief that Bennett's teams can't win in March.

Like Valvano said, when you get on a roll, who knows.

Guy certainly believed a championship could happen. He left the Sunday media session with a parting shot, pointing out that after the UMBC loss to the national championship.

"We're looking for a '30 for 30.'"

# CHAPTER 10
# Manic Monday

Remember how De'Andre Hunter was having trouble scoring on Francisco Caffaro in warmups?

The shooting issues did lap over to the game. Hunter missed his first seven shots from the floor, and had just one make in the first half, with 1:30 to go.

Trying to find the positive: he was, at least, aggressive, which had also been an issue for Hunter in the NCAA Tournament.

"My shots just weren't falling," said Hunter, whose poor shooting didn't affect the Cavaliers, early on, anyway.

CHRIS GRAHAM

CHRIS GRAHAM

UVA built a 17-7 lead prior to an 18-4 answer from Texas Tech that gave the Red Raiders a 25-21 advantage with 4:50 to go until halftime.

The 'Hoos closed strong, finishing with an 11-4 run — punctuated by a Ty Jerome three to beat the buzzer that was set up by Hunter, and UVA went into the locker room up 32-29.

The second half started out well for Virginia, as it had in the semifinal win over Auburn. The Cavaliers led by as many as 10, at 53-43, on a Kyle Guy three with 10:24 to go.

It was still an eight-point UVA lead after Hunter converted an offensive rebound from a Guy miss with 5:46 left.

Hunter missed the free throw that could have made it an and-one and pushed the margin to nine.

The Auburn game had turned at a similar stage after the boneheaded foul by Jerome helped ignite a 14-0 Tigers run.

There was nothing of that nature precipitating the 8-0 run by Texas Tech over the next 2:24 that tied the game at 59.

There were only seven possessions total in that stretch. Virginia missed two shots and had a turnover, by Hunter, that the Red Raiders weren't able to convert into points.

But a jumper by Kyler Edwards, a three by Matt Mooney and an and-one by Norense Odiase knotted the game.

A pair of Mamadi Diakite free throws at the 2:56 mark put Virginia back on top. Jarrett Culver, struggling all night on his way to a 5-for-22, 15-point effort, rebounded his own miss and was fouled by Guy on the stickback, and made both ends to tie the score at 61 with 2:38 left.

A Hunter pull-up jumper made it 63-61 UVA with 2:21 to go.

Culver missed a three on Texas Tech's next possession, and then Guy hit a driving layup on a nice assist from Braxton Key to make it 65-61 Virginia with 1:44 on the clock.

Before UVA fans could exhale, though, Davide Moretti drained one from 25 feet 11 seconds later.

Virginia 65, Texas Tech 64.

Hunter's only miss of the second half was a blocked shot by Odiase with 1:09 to go.

Brandone Francis missed a three with 44 seconds left, but a jump-ball was called on the ensuing rebound, which had appeared, originally, to have been corralled by Guy, but TV replays showed later that Guy and Culver had, indeed, both possessed the ball simultaneously.

Guy, wrestling for the ball with Culver, fell backward with some force, and his head bounced off the floor.

Texas Tech inbounded, and Culver, draped by Hunter, at the free-throw line, spun to his left, drop-stepped, and converted a twisting, left-handed layup, with 35 seconds left, to put Texas Tech on top, 66-65.

Chris Beard called a 30-second timeout. Virginia, out of the timeout, ran a play for Jerome that was one of the go-to plays for the Cavaliers in late-game situations, overloading the right side of the floor to give Jerome a one-on-one on the left side.

Jerome seemed to have trouble deciding whether to use glass or shoot it straight at the rim, and the shot went long, with 22 seconds left.

Odiase rebounded and was fouled, and the 63.6 percent free-throw shooter made both ends of the one-and-one.

Three-point game.

Virginia needed a reprise of the Elite Eight "play of the century."

One was in the offing, though, almost unfathomably, it almost didn't happen, because the guy who would drain the game-tying three didn't know the play call.

"[Coach Bennett] was just telling me the play that we were running, because I don't think I knew it," Hunter said of what happened as he ran to the corner, originally confused.

It was a similar play as the one that had Jerome missing on the short runner. This time around, the Texas Tech defense, inexplicably, crunched down on Jerome as he turned the corner into the lane, leaving Hunter open in the right corner.

Jerome found Hunter with a laser pass, and, wide open, he connected, with 12.9 seconds left, holding the pose on his follow-through for posterity.

The game was tied.

\*\*\*

The game also wasn't over yet.

The Red Raiders inbounded and attacked. Culver, who had come up big late after struggling all game long, launched a deep three with five seconds left that missed, and Hunter rebounded.

Guy, three feet away, tried to signal for timeout, but Hunter, for some reason, was trying to outlet the ball to Guy, instead of holding on to the ball.

In the confusion, the ball went out of bounds, off the 'Hoos.

After an official review of how much time should be on the clock, and a Texas Tech timeout, the Red Raiders inbounded the ball, to Culver, in the left corner.

Hunter was originally supposed to be on Culver, but he and Key, who had been assigned to guard the inbound pass, switched, so it was Key on Culver as the Big 12 Player of the Year twisted in the air to try to get a long three off at the buzzer.

Key blocked the shot, and …

We were in overtime.

\*\*\*

Hunter got it started with a pair of freebies before the Red Raiders got five straight points out of Mooney, a three-ball followed by a shot that he flipped up that bounced around and in, giving his team a 73-70 edge with 3:08 to go.

Guy was tripped by Moretti, putting the Cavaliers in the double bonus, on the ensuing trip, and Mr. Ice Water in his Veins sank two to trim it to a point.

Then, after a Moretti miss on the other end, Hunter put the 'Hoos ahead to stay with a three from just about the same spot as the one he hit to send it to OT, and UVA led 75-73 with 2:09 remaining.

Diakite emphatically blocked a Culver runner, then Mooney missed badly from three, giving Virginia the ball and the lead inside of a minute and a half to go.

Jerome missed on a mid-range jumper, and the loose ball tracked all the way to the backcourt, where it was picked up by Moretti.

Hunter got his hand in as Moretti struggled to get a handle on the ball down the right sideline, and the ball went out of bounds.

The call was Texas Tech ball, but Hunter signaled to the bench to request a replay review.

On the TV broadcast, the CBS team of Jim Nantz, Bill Raftery and Grant Hill initially agreed with the call on the court. It was Nantz, on a later viewing, as officials Ron Groover, Michael Stephens and Terry Wymer huddled around a TV monitor at the scorer's table across the court, who was first to notice that it appeared that the ball had last been in contact with Moretti's right pinkie.

Additional views for the TV viewers at home seemed to cement that fact, and eventually, the game officials agreed, and signaled a reversal.

Virginia ball.

Jerome got around Mooney on a drive into the lane and was fouled, and just missed on the layup that would have given him a chance at the and-one.

He made both free throws to extend the lead to 77-73 with 41 seconds left.

Francis missed a makeable three nine seconds later, and Key rebounded, was fouled, and went 2-for-2 at the line to make it 79-73 Virginia with 31 ticks on the clock.

Culver, no other way to say it, blinked, misfiring on a misguided 27-foot three with 27 seconds left.

Diakite snared the rebound, and made two more free throws, and it was 81-73 with 23 seconds remaining.

Edwards made an uncontested driving layup at the 17-second mark to get the margin back to six, and Beard called a 30-second timeout to set up his defense.

Bennett, on the Virginia sideline, drew up an inbounds play that sent Key, alone, streaking into the frontcourt.

Jerome, the trigger, found him, and Key threw down the emphatic dunk with 15 seconds left, and reality was starting to set in.

Francis made another uncontested layup, Key was fouled on the inbounds, made two more free throws – Virginia would shoot 12-for-12 at the charity stripe in the extra period – and Mooney missed a meaningless three with four seconds left.

Hunter, fittingly, ended up with the rebound, and threw the ball into the sky as the final horn sounded.

Virginia 85, Texas Tech 77.

The Cavaliers were your 2019 national champions.

\*\*\*

As the confetti fell and that iconic tune started to play, Jack Salt slung his left arm over the shoulders of Kody Stattmann and his right over those of Jayden Nixon.

ZACH PERELES

CHRIS GRAHAM

Yes, Salt — he of 128 career games and more than 2,000 minutes as a Cavalier — slung his arms around two teammates who didn't have a big role this season as "One Shining Moment" began to play on the big screen.

He didn't seek out the players he'd shared the court with Monday. He didn't seek out the coach who had started recruiting him six years ago.

He didn't need to.

"All the players, the managers, the coaches, we're all on the same level," Salt said. "We all work as hard as we can to help achieve a goal, and that's to be the best we can. To finish with a national championship is a credit to everyone."

In the wake of Virginia's loss to UMBC in 2018, the Cavaliers had adopted the motto "United Pursuit." In the coming months, Bennett would add other words — taken from the Bible, from TED Talks, from books, from other people.

"United Pursuit" remained above all others.

The Cavaliers were national champs not because they did anything extraordinary. Yes, they had players who made difficult shots, who make perfect passes, who protected their own basket like their lives depended on it – and in Bennett's system, they pretty much do.

But they didn't change. They didn't falter. They didn't panic.

"[Our mindset was] just to remain faithful to the little things," Jerome said. "Coach Bennett always talks about staying faithful, and he told us,

'Don't grow weary in doing good,' and that's an every-possession mindset. It's a life mindset.

"Just play 'til that buzzer sounds."

\*\*\*

Hunter had dreamed of having the ball in his hands as the buzzer sounded on a Virginia national championship.

"That's just something I always wanted to do," Hunter said after the game. "I said, 'If I win a championship, I'm gonna have the ball, and I'm gonna throw it up as high as I can,' and it came true tonight."

Hunter picked a perfect time to have his best game as a Cavalier. The final statline is outstanding: a career-high 27 points on just 16 shots and nine rebounds to go alongside. The circumstances it came under make it even more impressive, because it certainly didn't look like it would be a career night for the redshirt sophomore at the jump.

He missed a layup right at the rim on his first shot. He was off the mark on a mid-range jumper — his bread and butter — on his second attempt. By halftime, he had made just one of his eight shots. And this was nothing new; Hunter had struggled mightily all tournament with his normally reliable jumper and his ability to attack the basket.

In that moment, as Virginia sat in the locker room leading 32-29, it seemed like the Cavaliers might need to find a way to survive another round without their top individual talent on top of his game.

Hunter had other plans. He would change the results, but he would, like the rest of his team, not change his composed approach.

"I wasn't angry," Hunter said. "I was just playing loose. I wasn't getting upset that I was missing. … In the second half, I just wanted to continue to do what I was doing in the first half. I felt like in the first half, I was being aggressive. My shots just weren't falling, and I knew in the second half, if I kept doing the same thing, they were gonna start to fall, and they did."

What happened over the next 25 minutes, though, was more than just shots falling. It was Hunter — the player who made this Virginia team different because he is such a great one-on-one player and next-level talent — saving his team.

The rim, much less Texas Tech, proved no worthy adversary as he splashed down jumpers and muscled his way to the basket, rarely even drawing iron on his shots. Hunter scored 17 points in the second half and five more in overtime.

No points were more important than the corner three he nailed to force overtime, though.

ZACH PERELES

And, remember, he didn't even know the ball was supposed to come his way.

When it did find his hands, off a perfect pass from a driving Jerome, Hunter had one thought.

"I was like, 'I have to make this,'" Hunter said. "That's exactly what I said in my head, and I shot it. It felt good, it was on line, and it went in."

Without Jerome, one of college basketball's great passers, that ball doesn't get there.

Then again, without Jerome speaking at halftime, Hunter never even gets involved in the game.

"Ty just told me, he loves aggressive me," Hunter said. "He's confident in me all the time, but just having that confidence going into the second half, I just knew I could be aggressive, and nothing bad could come of it."

This wasn't out of the ordinary, though. At Louisville during the regular season, Hunter sat for much of the first half with two fouls. When he came back a self-described "angry" version of himself, he scored 18 in the second half on his way to a 26-point afternoon.

That version, though this time not fueled by anger, reappeared in the title game. Hunter's outstanding performance isn't one that will soon be forgotten. Hunter dove fully, for the final time this season, into another one of Bennett's key phrases: "The joy is in the competition." He repeated those words in his press conference, a smile coming to his face.

"I was really just having fun," Hunter said. "It was probably the most fun I've had all year, especially for this stage and all that was on the line."

\*\*\*

They won because of a text Key received while sitting in Greek Art History class.

The NCAA hadn't yet cleared Key, a transfer from Alabama, for immediate eligibility, and the season opener was just days away.

"Coach Bennett texted me and said, 'Hey, give me a call,' and my heart kind of dropped, because I kind of knew what it was," Key said. "I was like, 'Hopefully it's good news.'

"I called him after class, and it was great news."

It was great news for Key, who had applied for a hardship waiver to allow an ill family member to see him play immediately, and for Virginia, which used his defensively versatility, physicality and quickness throughout the year and again in the championship game.

In 28 minutes, Key had six points, a team-high 10 rebounds, two assists and a big-time block.

Virginia outscored Texas Tech by 18 with him on the floor.

Key's playing time — like that of his fellow role players — had fluctuated throughout the year. He had played 10 minutes against Auburn and just two against Purdue.

But he stayed ready.

"I kind of figured I'd play a lot," Key said. "Before the game, [Bennett] doesn't really tell you, but I just knew with their physicality and how big they were, how strong they were, I might have a chance to play. I was thankful to play a little bit today; made my day."

Virginia's role players were key all year, though — not just in the finale. Key came through in crucial junctures when Virginia needed size, versatility and rebounding on the wing. Salt provided outstanding defense against big, physical post players. Diakite became Virginia's go-to big man and hit the shot against Purdue that saved the season. Kihei Clark bothered opposing guards all year long and hit several important shots. Jay Huff provided an offensive and shot-blocking boost when called upon.

While Hunter, Jerome and Guy provided the top-shelf skill any team needs to compete at a high level, the players around them provided the versatility needed to win a championship.

And while the Big Three rightfully drew most of the headlines, it was Key who provided the exclamation point with a breakaway dunk. Before the season started, he didn't even know if he'd play at all this season. He ended up putting the cherry on top of it.

"I'm just so blessed," Key said.

\*\*\*

They won because of a coach who never wavered in his system or his beliefs or his faith. There's another phrase Bennett loves to use that shows how his consistent approach bred a consistent program: "Don't grow weary in doing good; for at the due time, you'll reap a harvest." This year's team embraced that one, too.

"These guys have been so faithful this year, and that's been such a joy to me," Bennett said on the eve of the championship game. "And the players I've been under, when they faced adversity in a basketball sense — I'm not talking about a world sense, a basketball sense — they haven't grown weary in doing the right stuff."

Bennett didn't lose faith in his approach when Virginia suffered disappointment after disappointment or even when they suffered historic defeat. He, like any great coach, made adjustments to fit his personnel where he saw fit, but his core principles remained grounded in defense and efficient, opportunistic offense.

The 85-77 scoreline doesn't change that.

Virginia averaged 1.21 points per possession in a 70-possession overtime game. That's right where the Cavaliers wanted the pace to be, and their multifaceted offensive attack made each possession count.

Jerome, Guy and Hunter — the three faces of the program, all part of the star 2016 recruiting class — combined for 67 points.

"To see them come either in as young men or boys and grow into men, this season, I'll mention what happened last year — that can only mature you," Bennett said. "I don't know of anything else that would allow these guys to be able to handle this situation, to play through stuff and to have a perspective and a poise and a resiliency unless they went through something that hard.

"They're really good players. They don't probably get enough credit — well, I think some of them do — for their talent, but they had something different about them collectively."

Against one of the nation's premier defensive teams, especially on the interior, the Cavaliers lit it up from deep (11-for-24, 45.8 percent), a strength for them all year. Against one of the nation's most physical and aggressive defenses, the Cavaliers turned it over just 11 times, a testament to the preparation and play of Jerome, Guy and Clark.

On defense, Hunter and Key were terrific on Culver, a likely future NBA lottery pick, and Mooney, who had 22 against Michigan State in the semifinal.

"They gave great defense," Culver said. "They played the whole time, they all played hard, they played together."

There's that word again, "together." Bennett preached togetherness from the start with his "United Pursuit" motto. But as Monday night turned into Tuesday morning, he had another group he had to join, as he told Nantz.

"I can't wait to celebrate with my wife, my kids and my parents, and I do want to thank the Lord," Bennett said.

Those were the important ones. The ones who helped Bennett get to where he is and become the champion he is today. His dad was his coach, his sister a terrific athlete. He used faith-based quotes and applied them to the game of basketball, recognizing that not everyone shared his religiosity, but everyone shared his love for the game.

That's who Tony Bennett is. That's who Virginia is. And because of it, the Cavaliers were taking their first-ever NCAA basketball championship trophy back to Charlottesville.

Why be anything other than yourself when you can do that?

# CHAPTER 11
# Celebrate!

Several notable Virginia alums were at U.S. Bank Stadium to be part of Cavalier basketball history on when the program captured its first NCAA national championship.

**KATIE COURIC (television journalist):** "This is so exciting. It was so stressful, but this team has so much heart. As Tony Bennett said, never lost faith, and honestly, it's magical to be able to be here and see them win a national championship for the first time. Charlottesville needs this."

**MALCOLM BROGDON (Milwaukee Bucks):** "It's amazing. It's surreal to watch these guys, to be able to be a fan, root these guys on, and just, man, watch them accomplish greatness.

"Me, Joe [Harris], Devon [Hall], Anthony Gill, Akil Mitchell, Darion Atkins, guys like that, man — we all had a part in it, but cheering these guys on and supporting them is what we did this year. They pulled it out, and it was amazing.

"Man, it was nerve-wracking. I was nervous, but I knew we would pull it out once we got into overtime. All we needed to do was tie the game up and go into overtime. It was UVA's year for sure."

ZACH PERELES

**JUSTIN ANDERSON (Atlanta Hawks):** "Unbelievable. It's an amazing feeling. These guys deserve this, and it's so great to be a part of this. This is an unbelievable experience for everyone that's a part of the program. I'm just super proud right now."

Anderson talked about being part of the teams that helped build the foundation that led to a championship.

"It's a big foundation. Obviously, we believe in the pillars and Coach Bennett, and what he's instilled in us, my teammates. This is just a surreal moment, and we're all just so proud and happy for the group that finally got a chance to do it.

"This showed our preparation, and it shows our poise, our character. These guys were prepared, and it really showed in the end."

**CARLA WILLIAMS (University of Virginia Athletics Director):** "It means so much. It's really hard to describe what it means. I'm so very happy for Tony, for his staff, for these players, that went through so much adversity last year — and they were champions last year, in my mind. The way they handled that adversity made them champions, and so this is just kind of the crowning victory for everything that they've been through for the last year. Very proud, so very proud.

"You know what? It was nerve-wracking, but deep down I always feel like we'd find a way to win, because I did feel like we were destined to win it. Even though I was nervous, deep down I always felt like we would win."

**CHRIS LONG (Philadelphia Eagles):** "It means everything as a fan. It's almost like you have as much invested in being a fan as being a player, so this is the time that I get to really just live and die with it.

"You know what? Tonight, I felt a real calm, because we got off to a good start, we were getting good looks the whole first half, so I felt like if they stop hitting threes — which they really didn't for a while — and we continued to get those looks, we were going to be fine.

"It was absolutely a long time coming."

**TIKI BARBER (CBS Sports national radio and TV talk show host):** "Well, I know it means more to them, but for me as an alum, this is a real sense of satisfaction. UVA has always been close, but never there. Doing things the right way, fighting through resiliency and bad things that sometimes happen, like losing to a 16-seed, keep plugging — and Tony's instilled a resiliency and a determination in these guys. It's just, it's inspiring. It really is."

Tiki addressed whether Virginia was a "Team of Destiny."

"You hate to put fate as the cause, but when everything seemed to be going awry, even in the Final Four game against Auburn, most of us had our heads down and would've counted that as a loss, and a miracle happened. Maybe it was a missed call on the double-dribble, but Kyle calmly drilled three free throws to send us here, and they took care of business."

\*\*\*

The win set off a wild celebration at the John Paul Jones Arena, which was as rollicking with the game on the big screen as it has ever been for a live basketball game; to The Lawn, where students had watched the game on a projector screen at the amphitheater; to The Corner, which was packed with fans taking in the game at bars and restaurants, to the Downtown Mall, where fans filled the historic Paramount Theater.

SCOTT GERMAN

SCOTT GERMAN

Thousands lined the route from the Charlottesville-Albemarle Airport to JPJ as the team arrived back in Charlottesville the next day, flooring Bennett, who admitted to not being totally aware of what had been going on back home as the team battled in Minneapolis.

"I don't know if it's really sunk in yet," Bennett said at the next-day meet-and-greet. "But when we were driving here, and the fans along the road [showed] what it means to them, that's one of the good things about sports — how it brings a community together.

"Everybody wants to be a part of something bigger than themselves, and this has been remarkable. It is an amazing story. ... This community has embraced our guys and what they represent. And to be able to bring them joy is as good as it gets."

The official welcome-home event was set for the weekend, at Scott Stadium, and it drew an estimated 21,000 fans on a rainy afternoon, as if rain was going to stop Wahoo Nation from coming out in force.

If anyone knows how to weather a storm, it's this group of fans and the team for which they cheered.

Wahoo legend Ralph Sampson and Voice of the Cavaliers Dave Koehn got things started a little after 2 p.m.,

CRYSTAL GRAHAM

as the clouds lifted, and the sun shone bright, with Sampson taking a question from Koehn about when it was that Sampson had decided he would sit courtside as the basketball team made its way from Columbia, S.C., to Minneapolis.

"I decided it 40 years ago," Sampson said to an ovation. "Ironically, 40 years ago today was my official visit, this weekend, to the University of Virginia. It's my mother's birthday, she turns 81 today, so it was 40 years ago that I came here on my official visit and decided to go to UVA. So, how special is this 40 years later?"

Sampson admitted that he wore the same pair of shoes to all six NCAA Tournament games, that he now plans to "retire" until a later date.

"I'm going to wear them next year so we can do it twice," Sampson exclaimed, which drew an even louder roar.

Koehn later asked Williams if she had thought such a scene was possible when she took the job in 2017.

"My answer was, 'Absolutely,'" Williams said. "I believe that sports brings people together, all kinds of people, and this team, our coaches, our players, has been a unifying force, not just for the athletic department, not just for the University, not just for Charlottesville, but for the Commonwealth of Virginia. And for that, I am thankful."

CRYSTAL GRAHAM

CRYSTAL GRAHAM

Bennett, a few days into having had a chance to process what had happened, and what the national championship meant to the community, the fan base, told a story about the moment from earlier in the season at Clemson.

"We're riding up on the bus, and it was the time where they were going to celebrate the football national championship. And we're riding up on the bus, and the stadium's full, and we're getting ready for a noon game, and I remember thinking, 'Man, what would that be like if we ever won a national championship?'"

He paused.

"And you know what? That day is now!" he roared, then pumped his fist with a satisfying laugh, high-fiving his players and displaying the excitement of a kid waking up on Christmas morning.

"Our theme was 'United Pursuit,' because we knew it would be that," Bennett told Wahoo fans young and old, "and I can't help but think this is a united celebration of that pursuit. I'm blown away by it. You hope for something like this, but this is beyond what I expected."

Bennett thought back to his early days on the job, when his first order of business was selling the players that he'd inherited from predecessor Dave Leitao on his way of doing things.

"I've got a poster of 'Rocky,' I said it after the game, we just wanted a chance at a title fight, and that was the hope," Bennett said.

"To be here with you guys, and how you've embraced us, is special. So, I've got to be honest, I never expected anything like this, if I'm truthful. … This is making it real, that's for sure."

Kihei Clark and Mamadi Diakite talked about their respective roles in "The Play of the Century," Braxton Key touched on his game-saving block at the end of regulation against Texas Tech, while Jack Salt reflected on being the lone senior, his program-record 118 wins at UVA, his future professional plans, and most of all, the memories.

"This has been amazing," Salt said. "I've had the opportunity to be a part of a great team, I've met some of my best friends for life being at this school, and thanks to Coach Bennett for letting me come here. I've had an amazing experience."

De'Andre Hunter admitted that he didn't play his best basketball throughout the tournament, but explained that he knew he had to step up and be aggressive when it mattered most, including his three-pointer late in regulation that sent the title game to overtime.

"I was honestly hoping that Ty [Jerome] would pass the ball," Hunter joked, with Jerome looking on with a grin. "He was shooting a lot, he was shooting those floaters, so he passed it to me in the corner, it was a good pass, I was in rhythm, and it's a shot that I shoot all the time in practice, so I just had to knock it down."

Final Four Most Outstanding Player Kyle Guy told the fans about the pressure-packed moments leading up to his game-clinching free throws against Auburn.

"We just tried to buckle down and be as disciplined as possible," Guy said. "We were laser-focused all of March, and we did a great job executing and just never giving up, even though we were down in some instances, and we did our job."

Jerome pointed out where he got his motivation to help lead the program to its first title.

"Just wanting to win so bad," he said, "with my teammates, with these coaches, for these fans — just wanting to win and just all the work we've put in. … It was a dream come true."

Cavalier redshirt-freshman forward Francesco Badocchi showed off the piano skills that had helped lighten the mood for his teammates in games of "Name That Tune," putting the finishing touches on the ceremony with a rendition of "One Shining Moment."

It was a tune that everybody on hand could name before the first note.

\*\*\*

For a day, it certainly was a dream come true — or perhaps a dream realized as true once again.

That the event was even held at Scott Stadium, rather than at JPJ, which

CRYSTAL GRAHAM

was hosting an event, was a dream come true for Bennett, a dream that took a decade 10 years to realize.

"When I first got the job, there was a Dave Matthews concert going on, and I remember, I was maybe a week on the job, in my office, and I just snuck out, and I looked at the stadium, and I remember saying, 'Someday it's gonna be like this for basketball,'" Bennett said at a press conference that followed the celebration.

"And then to walk out here. They said we can't do it at JPJ. … They said it won't be able to hold enough people. And I was like, 'Come on, there's gonna be enough room in there.'"

For what it's worth, Bennett would have been wrong.

JPJ holds roughly 15,000.

"This community has been through a lot, and then to see this come together and celebrate with them, it was a united celebration," Bennett said, harkening back to the team's "United Pursuit" motto.

"Nothing else mattered but celebrating this."

For Guy, the magnitude of the championship was only beginning to hit him. He's had to stay after class to grant picture requests and had talked to plenty of media outlets since the victory.

But he still was "kind of at a loss for words for what we've accomplished."

Bennett shared in that feeling.

"I don't think, really, it has sunk in," Bennett said. "It's just little things like this. … I just think it'll get better and better."

Ahead of the national championship game the previous Monday, Virginia went through its walkthrough to the tune of one of the songs it has used all season, Andy Grammer's "Back Home."

In the hook, Grammer sings: "And no matter where we go, we always find our way back home."

The Cavaliers did find their way back home, and their fans had followed them there.

\*\*\*

At 3:05 p.m., a little more than an hour after the event had started, the celebration was over.

Players and coaches were leaving the stage, and the fans that had flocked in would just as quickly find the exits in the following minutes as well.

Some traveled great distances to get here.

Others had walked down the street.

But for one afternoon, they all had called Scott Stadium their home, even if for just a few hours, alongside their fellow fans, the team and coaches that led them to a championship and a trophy that finds its home, for the first time, in Charlottesville, Va.

# PART II
# The Championship Team

# TONY BENNETT
## A great believer

*"Out of suffering have emerged the strongest souls; the most massive characters are seared with scars."* – Kahilil Gibran

Tony Bennett is a great believer that in order to appreciate the highest of highs, one must experience the lowest of lows. Nothing better describes Bennett's Virginia basketball team over the past two years more than the quote above from the philosopher Gibran.

March 2018, Bennett and his Cavaliers were in a dark place, having suffered the lowest of lows. Ranked No. 1 in the nation for much of the season, Virginia entered the NCAA Tournament as the country's top overall seed. The Cavaliers were stunned in the first round by No. 16 seed UMBC, the first time in tournament history that a No. 16 shocked a No. 1.

Little more than a year later, Virginia fulfilled its quest as a "Team of Destiny," by overcoming improbable odds in its last three games to capture the program's first national championship.

From worst to first in one year's time set off unprecedented celebrations across Wahoo Nation in a gigantic sigh of relief so strong that it could have blown the Nina, the Pinta, and the Santa Maria across the Atlantic. Bourbon stock must have gone through the roof.

"Redemption" was the theme.

Virginia legend Ralph Sampson said it best at the national championship celebration back in Charlottesville's Scott Stadium after the title game.

"It's the greatest story in the history of college basketball," said Sampson, the three-time National Player of the Year from an era gone by.

Who is going to disagree?

Certainly not another legend, CBS commentator Jim Nantz, who called his 29th consecutive Final Four, and pointed out prior to the start of the championship weekend that should Virginia pull off such a feat after experiencing the doom of a year prior, it would symbolize one of the greatest

JON GOLDEN

turnarounds in years, not only in just college basketball, but in all sports.

One of March Madness' most tragic victims, UVA's Kyle Guy, someone tormented, yet inspired by that abysmal defeat to UMBC, poetically summed up those emotions.

"That's a dark path that I think a lot of us were on," Guy explained the process following the Cavaliers' glorious comeback to claim the title over Texas Tech in overtime. "It was humiliation, embarrassment for ourselves, and our families and the program. To be able to redeem all that and get this program something that's never happened before is all that I could ever want."

For the Cavaliers to pull off three consecutive implausible victories under the immense pressure of the Elite Eight (Purdue in overtime), the national semifinal (Auburn), then in the championship (Texas Tech in overtime), made believers of everyone that this was a team of destiny.

How else could one explain the Kihei Clark-to-Mamadi Diakite tip-pass-shot play that sent the Purdue game into overtime? Or, Guy getting fouled in the corner on a three-point attempt at game's end, and him making three pressure-packed free throws to win the game? Or De'Andre Hunter's three-pointer with 12 seconds to go that sent UVA's game with the Red Raiders into overtime, where

JON GOLDEN

the Cavaliers made all dozen of its free throws en route to the crown?

*The Wall Street Journal*'s research revealed that the odds of Virginia pulling off back-to-back-to-back wins under those circumstances were a whopping 1-in-2,500. Looking back, most Wahoo fans would argue more like one in a million.

Fate, fortune, karma, kismet? Perhaps.

Bennett a man who proudly wears his strong faith and is never reluctant to say so, believed there was another intervention.

"I think there was a bigger plan going on here, and I didn't need it, but I was used in it," the Virginia coach said in his final statement before he exited the championship podium that unforgettable night at U.S. Bank Stadium in Minneapolis. "I hope that it's a message for some people out there that there can be hope and joy and resiliency. I'm thankful for what happened, and that's why I did what I did at the end."

When the Cavaliers' magical ride ended, and the horn sounded, and the confetti began to fall from the heavens, Bennett put his head down and thanked his Maker.

"I'm humbled, Lord, because I don't deserve to be in this spot, but You chose me to be here, and I'll give thanks," Bennett shared with media in the postgame interview.

\*\*\*

The Virginia coach had repeated his thoughts on the Final Four over the past few seasons. Yes, he had a burning desire to get there, having gotten a taste of it as a graduate assistant under his father, Dick Bennett, at Wisconsin 19 years hence. No, it was not going to make or break his career or his life if Tony Bennett never got there.

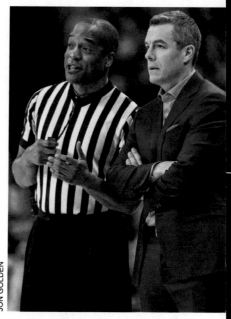

Most college coaches probably wouldn't agree with that theory. For many, reaching the Final Four, especially winning it all, is the pinnacle of their existence. Some will do most anything, breaking rules, looking the other way, accepting players with shady reputations, to get there. Not Tony Bennett. He doesn't believe in shortcuts or doing anything inappropriate for the sake of winning.

While getting to the Final Four was a sweet accomplishment, and winning it all was even more so, it wasn't his end all. That philosophy was adapted from a moment when his dad made it to basketball heaven and realized that it wasn't heaven at all.

"I remember 19 years ago, I was sitting in the back of a press conference. My father took his team to the Final Four. They beat Purdue. I memorized his quote. He said a quote I never forgot. It stuck with me for that long.

"[Media] asked him: is this one of the greatest feelings that you've ever had, getting to the Final Four? He said this: from a feeling state, euphoria, yes, it is. But it doesn't compare with faith, with kids, family, grandkids. He said, 'Because I know what truly matters, it enables me to enjoy what seems to matter.'"

Pause and think about that last sentence for a moment, and you'll understand everything you need to know about Tony and Dick Bennett. Tony has tried to live by that quote for the rest of his life.

"I want this program to honor what's important to me, my faith and these young men through success and through failure," Tony Bennett explained. "As a competitor, you go after it, and you want to do it, but in the bigger picture, you have to be at peace with both."

\*\*\*

Any media person will tell you that Bennett does not love these press conferences. He seeks no limelight for himself. If he has any ego at all, it only comes out in any type of competition one might challenge him on (ask all his former and present assistants about his relentless competitive fire). Long press conferences are a form of torture for a man whom everyone can't get enough of.

At one point during a 30-minute media chat along the way, Bennett kept looking at his watch and commented to the moderator that it seemed like he'd been up on the podium for an awfully long time. While postgame media responsibilities usually last 10 minutes or less, the NCAA requires coaches for longer periods of time, much to Bennett's chagrin.

However, when the Virginia coach opens up, he often delivers golden fodder for sportswriters across the land.

After the championship win over Texas Tech, Bennett revisited the past year's journey and gave his own version of what his father had said nearly two decades ago.

He was asked if the pain of UMBC had gone away.

"Yeah, I mean, you have scars, right?" Bennett replied. (Somewhere Gibran is smiling.) "You have a scar, and it reminds you, but it's a memory. Does it go away completely? No, I wish it wouldn't have happened in some ways. Now I say, well, it bought us a ticket here. So be it."

His response was almost as eloquent and certainly as heartfelt as the year before when he gained national popularity with the way he gracefully handled the upset loss.

But Bennett wasn't through with his thoughts about picking up the hardware for the UVA trophy case.

"I'm thankful in a way for what happened [UMBC], because it did, it drew me closer, most importantly, to my faith in the Lord, drew me closer to my wife and children, just because you realize what's unconditional. In those spots, when the world's telling you you're a failure, you're a loser, and you're the worst thing going, and all that stuff, you say, OK, what really matters? And it pushed me to that in a way."

Pushed, then drove Bennett. He said the early exit the year before ignited a larger fire in his belly to get this team, to get Virginia, to the Final Four. He and his staff took on a challenge to find answers for perhaps any obstacle that might get in their way of that goal, and openly talked about it instead of running away.

"Is the pain gone? I still feel a little, 'Uhh,' because I remember that feeling, but I think we're OK."

\*\*\*

Perhaps *everything* became OK that late night in Louisville after the Cavaliers had pulled off another wonder over Purdue. Over his 10-year coaching reign at Virginia, no one had ever witnessed such outward jubilation from Bennett.

After climbing the ladder to snip the final strand of championship net from the South Regional victory, the Cavaliers' coach turned toward his team and the crowd, raising both fists triumphantly into the air and let out a mighty roar.

It was as if all the pressure from a decade of criticism released in that powerful exhale from the top of the ladder.

Pundits had said Virginia could never get to the Final Four playing "Bennett Ball," that his slow tempo style was boring and bad for college basketball, that his offense couldn't generate enough points to win it all, that his teams always choked under the pressure of postseason play.

Cut-throat opposing coaches would negatively recruit against Bennett's system, something he pointed out more than a year earlier when he told media, "They told prospects that if you go to Virginia, you'll never win an ACC title. Well, we proved that wasn't true. They said if you go to Virginia, you'll never have a chance at the NBA. We've proven that's not true. They said, if you go to Virginia, Tony's not going to be there when you graduate. He's going to leave for a bigger job. Well, *geesh, I've been here nine years.* What do I have to do?"

Critics certainly can't use the lack of a Final Four or national championship as recruiting ammunition anymore. Those are checked off the list, too.

Ask most any knowledge basketball person in the country, and they'll answer without hesitation that Bennett is one of the very best coaches in the nation. Still, there were observers that would always point out, "Well, he's never been to the Final Four," a take that some use in another sport: the best player to have never won a major (golf title).

That label was also peeled away in Louisville, then again in Minneapolis at game's end, when the tradition of placing a team's name into the winner's spot on the NCAA bracket – usually an honor reserved for a player – was all Bennett's.

He took the sticker that read "Virginia" and slapped it on the bracket, then slapped it several more times for good measure, as Wahoo fans went wild.

Finally, their moment had arrived. "One Shining Moment" that will never be forgotten.

It was a moment everyone thought was coming in 2016 when Virginia blew a huge second-half lead in the Midwest Regional finals in Chicago and lost to an underdog Syracuse team.

Ever since Bennett came to Charlottesville, he's had this "Rocky" Balboa poster in his office, because all he has wanted was a chance at a title fight, just like the movie's character. Syracuse was a late-round knockout, ending yet another Cavalier dream. But "Rocky" was a story of comebacks, and so was Virginia.

CHRIS GRAHAM

During this year's drive to the championship, Bennett reflected on that setback in Chicago and the one in Charlotte in 2018. After Chicago, he quoted from Psalms: "Joy will come in the morning." What carried through last year in Charlotte?

"There's a scripture verse that says, 'Always be prepared to give a reason for the hope that you have, but do it with gentleness and respect,'" Bennett said. "Everybody is at a different place with what they believe and where they're at, but when you're put in a spot like that, and there's a lot worse things, it makes you rely upon what matters. I said what's unconditional in my life.

"For me, that's my relationship with my wife, my parents, my kids, but the greatest joy that I know is my relationship with the Lord. Sometimes when you get knocked down, in a way, you find out how real that is. There's a perspective in it and a peace that is not really of the man-made stuff we're talking about."

Minneapolis had a different ending as Bennett received endless congratulations from around the globe, including a tweet from another coach that had once felt Bennett's pain, Villanova's Jay Wright. He had come under the same scrutiny for years and finally watched it all melt away after winning the championship.

Since then, *Fortune* magazine had named Bennett one of its 50 greatest world leaders. UVA athletic director Carla Williams already knew that. So did her two predecessors who lured Bennett clear across the country to set a new direction for Virginia basketball. Former AD Craig Littlepage and his associate AD Jon Oliver delivered an amazing sales pitch to pull off one of the greatest hiring coups in the history of the sport.

It is hard to forget Oliver's quote when he broke the news about Bennett's hiring.

JOHN MARKON

"This guy is a younger Krzyzewski," Oliver said, referring to the Duke coach who had become the winningest coach in college basketball history.

Oliver was right, and then some.

\*\*\*

Ten years later, in the locker room of the new national champions, Bennett had one more mission on his agenda. After all the celebrating, after media left the room, he shared one last, but important thought.

"I told our guys, 'Put your arms around each other, take a look at every guy in here. Look at each other. Promise me you will remain humble and thankful for this. Don't let this change you. It doesn't have to. We'll have memories. We'll be at each other's weddings. But stay humble and stay thankful. It's a great story.' That's probably the best way I can end this. It's a great story."

A story for the ages.

# KYLE GUY
## Composed when it counts

The task of selecting the turning point of Virginia's postseason march to the national championship would be challenging and hotly debated.

Would it be the Cavaliers' shaking off the remnants of last year's shocking upset after a sluggish first half against another No. 16 seed in Gardner-Webb? Or how about Kihei Clark's amazing pass to Mamadi Diakite for a buzzer-beating shot that sent the Purdue game into overtime, where UVA survived and advanced to the Final Four?

Then there was Kyle Guy's three-pointer late against Auburn, shortly followed by his three pressure-packed free throws to beat the Tigers

JOHN MARKON

and move on to the championship. In that title game, there was De'Andre Hunter's clutch three-pointer and Braxton Key's block of Texas Tech's Jarrett Culver, sending that game into overtime, where the Wahoos would eventually prevail.

Certainly, all those things had to occur in order for Virginia to bring the national championship trophy home to Charlottesville.

However, think back to the Elite Eight game against Purdue, and think again about Guy. Had the junior sharpshooter not emerged from a dismal shooting slump, those forthcoming miracles may never have materialized.

Guy was mired in an abysmal nose-dive from three-point range when he arrived at Louisville's KFC Yum! Center for a matchup against the

JON GOLDEN

Boilermakers. It was difficult to explain. He was the most accurate long-range bomber in UVA history, but in the three games leading up to Purdue, he couldn't throw a beach ball into the ocean.

In fact, his struggle continued through the first half against the Boilermakers, who led the Cavaliers 30-29 at the break. In victories over Gardner-Webb, Oklahoma and Oregon, combined with the first half against Purdue, Guy was an unfathomable 3-of-29 from the arc. That included one string of 16 consecutive misses during that span.

The former McDonald's All-American, the state of Indiana's "Mr. Basketball," couldn't buy one. He was 1-of-5 vs. Gardner-Webb, 0-of-10 against Oklahoma, 2-for-11 vs. Oregon, and 0-of-3 in the first half of the Purdue game.

Guy's streak was so baffling that both he and Tony Bennett were asked about it in an off-day press conference leading up to the Elite Eight game. How could this be? Was something wrong?

Guy, who would later say that he doesn't believe in slumps, replied that when his shots aren't falling, he tries to help the team in other ways, playing a little harder on defense or going for rebounds. He refused to be shaken. He never lost confidence.

"Just my presence on the floor sometimes gets guys open because [defenses] are not going to help off of me, even if I am shooting 0-for-10," Guy explained.

It is called shooter's amnesia, a short memory that discounts previous misses. A shooter's mentality means that no matter how many misses there are in a row, the belief is that the next one is going in.

Bennett understood this as well as anyone, because even though he still holds the NCAA's all-time record for career three-point shooting accuracy during his days at Wisconsin-Green Bay, he also knows, nobody's perfect.

"You've got to give Kyle freedom, because he's a moment away from getting it rolling," Bennett said. "He's so keyed upon [by defenses]. It's always noticeable for a shooter of his reputation when it's not going. As long as he's taking good shots, you give him that freedom."

Braxton Key, who shot his way out of a three-point slump in a win at Virginia Tech late in the season, understood Guy's woes.

"Kyle's confident. He's a shooter. Shooters are going to shoot. If you told him he missed 16, he'd be, 'OK, well, I'll make the next one.' That's the kind of confidence you've got to have, and speaks volumes about him as a player," Key said.

\*\*\*

JOHN MARKON

With only 2:09 remaining in the first half against Purdue, and the Cavaliers trailing 30-26, Wahoo Nation held its collective breath when Guy went down in a heap in front of press row and was writhing in pain.

Oh, no, was it a knee? An ankle? Was he done for the tournament?

Because Virginia teams have been haunted by serious injuries in previous seasons at the worst most possible times, it was understandable that Cavalier fans were more than nervous. If Guy was down for the count, how could UVA possibly fight off Purdue and red-hot Carsen

JON GOLDEN

Edwards, who would go on to score an amazing 42 points in the game, one of the most brilliant performances in tournament history?

Guy reflected upon the moment after the game, when he fought off the pain and came back to steal as much of Edwards' thunder as possible in leading the Cavalier comeback.

"I stepped on someone's foot, and I heard it pop," Guy said of his ankle. "That's kind of mostly why I was rolling around like I was, because I was really scared. But I thought what was best for me was to get up and let everybody know I was fine, and let Ethan [Saliba], our trainer, assess it."

Saliba, UVA's longtime trainer extraordinaire, worked his magic on Guy at halftime while Cavalier fans chewed off the remainder of their nails during the break. They were somewhat astonished when Guy came back into the arena for second-half warm-ups and looked like he was ready to go.

In what looked like another catastrophic moment for UVA hoops, *everything* changed for the good. Guy was more than ready to go. He was about to transform into the sharpshooter everyone knew.

Only 28 seconds passed by into the second half before Guy struck with a three-pointer from the top of the key and lifted the Cavaliers into the lead, 32-30. Less than a minute-and-a-half later, Guy delivered another dagger, this time from the right corner, and Virginia was up 35-30.

"Mr. Basketball" was back. He would go on to make 5-of-9 from behind the arc in the second half in a 25-point performance in which he connected on 8-of-19 field goal attempts and 4-of-5 from the free throw line. Had Guy not heated up, there wouldn't have been an opportunity for Clark and Diakite to send the game into overtime, where UVA eventually won, 80-75, and cut down the nets from the NCAA South Regional championship.

\*\*\*

When the buzzer sounded, sending Virginia to its first Final Four since 1984, it was a stark contrast to last March when Guy and teammates suffered a defeat that would haunt him for a year.

"I was definitely flashing back to when I was on my knees last year, and I did it again," Guy said.

This time it was for a very different reason.

"I was just overflowing with joy. So happy for my teammates and my coaches and for myself to be able to break through in the way that we did this year. Not only did we silence [Bennett's] critics, we silenced our own, and we're so grateful for our fans that traveled and have always believed in us."

Guy had rediscovered his rhythm and instead of taking credit, praised his teammates for continuing to look for him, ignoring his slump, but still screening for him and trusting that he would come through. His breakthrough in the second half against the Boilermakers signaled that nothing was going to slow him down the rest of the way, and nothing did.

From halftime vs. Purdue, and through the pair of Final Four games against Auburn and Texas Tech, Guy would make 11-of-24 attempts from three-point range (quite a contrast from the 3-of-29 in the previous three-and-a-half NCAA games leading up to that moment).

In addition, over the final three games, Purdue, Auburn, and Texas Tech, Guy would connect on 21-of-45 field goal attempts, 11-of-12 free throws, and score 64 points, and would be named Most Outstanding Player of the Final Four.

He rarely came off the floor, playing 41 minutes, 36 seconds against Purdue, 38:41 versus Auburn and the entire 45 minutes in the championship game with Texas Tech.

All the horror of the previous March and the anxiety that followed were a thing of the past. Guy, who openly admitted he had suffered from anxiety to begin with, and how the loss to UMBC only poured onto his problems, had dealt with all those issues. Bennett said that the best thing he could do for his star shooter during that entire year-long process was to pray for him.

Guy came to Virginia with the reputation of being a big-time shooter. His high school resume was impeccable, and Bennett knew he had landed a fierce competitor, a winner. While Guy was a bit scrawny when he showed up as a freshman, he could still shoot. Over time, Guy would add weight and muscle.

For some reason, he decided to sport a "man bun" his first year, which drew cat calls from opposing fans. But during those three seasons, he grew from Man Bun to The Man.

\*\*\*

No Wahoo worth his or her salt will ever forget the closing moments of the Auburn game in the Final Four semifinals.

Late in the second half, Virginia fell into a scoring funk after Ty Jerome's three-pointer with 5:21 to play. His trey had lifted the Cavaliers to a 10-point lead over the SEC's Tigers. That would be the last UVA points for the more than the five minutes that followed as Auburn stormed back and held a 61-57 lead with 17 seconds to play.

Things didn't look good for the Wahoos, at least not until Guy rode to the rescue. He sank a three-pointer from the right corner, narrowing Auburn's lead to a point at 61-60, with 7.4 seconds to play.

UVA's Clark fouled the Tigers' Harper, who made his first free throw, but missed the second. Because Auburn had fouls to give before Virginia would be in the one-and-one, Bruce Pearl ordered his players to foul the Cavaliers twice, reducing their chances of a miracle shot.

By then, Auburn had six team fouls and Virginia had less than two seconds to find a way to survive.

Jerome found Guy open in the left corner, and Guy launched a prayer that missed the mark. However, as Auburn started celebrating on the court and sidelines and Virginia players and fans were dejected, only few had noticed that game officials had whistled Auburn for a foul with *six-tenths* of a second remaining.

Official James Breeding ruled that the Tigers' Samir Doughty had "moved into the airborne shooter, making contact with Guy while taking away his landing spot."

Amid the Auburn protests, Guy was given three free throws, perhaps the most important Virginia free throws since Ralph Sampson's last home game

in University Hall, when he missed
his, then grabbed the rebound and
hit a short jumper for a victory over
Lefty Driesell's Maryland team.

JON GOLDEN

"I heard [the official] call it right
away," Guy said. "They were asking
me did I know, because I put my
face into my jersey, but that was me
focusing. I knew they called a foul.
I knew that I got behind the line for
three shots because I practice that.
I just literally told myself that we
dream of these moments, and to be
able to make one happen was special."

Guy made the first to cut Auburn's lead to 62-61. If he made the second,
UVA would at least force overtime. If he missed, he would have to make the
third, or the game would be over.

He sank the second, and Pearl immediately called timeout in hopes to
"freeze" Guy and multiply the pressure. During the timeout, Guy didn't join
the huddle with his teammates. He didn't want to talk to anyone, players or
coaches.

For a guy – pun intended – with anxiety issues, Guy couldn't have been any
more composed. Without flinching, he swished the third free throw for a 63-62
lead. Auburn would have essentially half a second to pull off its own miracle,
but a Tigers' Hail Mary wasn't even close, as Virginia's players and fans began a
frenzied celebration amidst the chorus of booing by upset Auburn fans.

Doughty, who was charged with the foul, did not complain about the call
after the game.

"They (the officials) do a great job at reffing, and they're trying to
the best of their ability to make the right call," the Tiger player said. "I
can't question none of that. I watched a lot of film on [Virginia's guards].
Kyle Guy and Ty Jerome like to kick their legs out when they shoot, so I
just tried to be right there, let him shoot the ball, and whatever happens,
happens. He just hit a three the play before, and I played defense the same
exact way. I'm not really sure why they called that call, but I'm pretty sure
the refs made the right decision."

Guy's three free throws may have been the biggest in Final Four history,
certainly in Wahoo history. Talk about clutch. Talk about pressure with 72,000
fans screaming at U.S. Bank Stadium, and everything on the line.

"I can't lie to you and say I knew I was going to hit them," Guy said later. "I
was terrified, but I had confidence in myself. This is what we dream of. For me

CHRIS GRAHAM

to be able to do this for our team, I couldn't be happier. I don't really have the words for how I feel, I really don't."

The Virginia sharpshooter had been pinching himself since arriving in Minneapolis, and so to put an ending together as he did, advancing the Cavaliers to the national championship game only added to the dream.

Bennett said that Guy's three at the end, then three free throws were terrific, and then paused before correcting himself.

"Terrific, sorry, that wasn't a strong enough word," the coach smiled. "Amazing, spectacular. I don't have many more. I didn't graduate from UVA, so my vocab is a little limited."

In the championship game against Texas Tech, Guy was spectacular, scoring 24 points and joining Hunter and Jerome on the All-Tournament team before being announced as the Most Outstanding Player.

That trio propelled the Cavaliers to their first national title, and in overtime, Guy hit all four free throws he attempted.

"I don't have the words to describe winning this championship," Guy said. "I'm so thankful for this team. I give all the glory to God and my family and my fiancée. They're the reason I'm here. They're the reason I'm here. This Most Outstanding Player does not belong to me. It belongs to this team, especially Ty and Dre."

The three Cavalier stars who arrived together three years ago and vowed they would make something special happen, then reiterated the faith to win a national championship in the aftermath of defeat the previous March, sat huddled together during the traditional "One Shining Moment."

# DE'ANDRE HUNTER
## Championship dreams come true

De'Andre Hunter had been thirsting for this his entire basketball-playing life.

After redshirting his first year at Virginia, then having suffered a broken wrist on the eve of the 2018 NCAA Tournament, he had been denied opportunities to participate in the Big Dance.

Once that moment arrived in March of 2019, Hunter put on his dancin' shoes and didn't take them off until he was wearing a crown.

Virginia was the king of college basketball, and if anyone was worthy of resting on the throne, it was Hunter.

JON GOLDEN

Had the redshirt sophomore not put his teammates on his back in the second halves of the Cavaliers' Final Four games, there would not have been any chances of miracle comebacks.

In the tournament games leading up to Minneapolis, Hunter's performances had been largely mediocre in terms of scoring. As hard as he tried, his shot just wasn't falling. While he focused on other parts of his game, including great defensive efforts, Virginia fans knew that, at some point, the Philly native was going to have to produce points if the Cavaliers were to win it all.

\*\*\*

The collective concern grew by halftime of the national semifinal game against Auburn. The Tigers, perhaps the hottest team in the tournament at that

JON GOLDEN

point, led UVA, 31-28 at halftime. Hunter had only two buckets and was 2-for-6 from the field.

If Virginia was to survive and advance to the championship game, then Hunter would have to emerge from the locker room at halftime and play like the NBA draft lottery pick he was projected to be.

That's exactly what Hunter did in igniting an 8-0 run to begin the second half. He quickly scored on a dunk as he took over the game early on. Attacking the basket, Hunter was fouled on a drive on UVA's next possession. Although he missed both free throws, he let the Tigers know that he was taking control.

He continued to attack, scored from inside on the Cavaliers' next possession, then blocked an Auburn shot on the other end, with Virginia regaining the lead at 34-31.

He wasn't through, scoring back-to-back minutes later, putting back the rebound of a missed three-pointer by Jerome, then scoring again inside the paint.

Hunter's relentless aggression allowed the Cavaliers to gain momentum, to answer Auburn's offense, and helped open up the floor for his teammates to score.

His final basket came with just under six minutes to play as he muscled his way through a Tiger double-team for another inside score and a 54-47 lead.

While his teammates finished the scoring from there, including Guy's momentous, game-winning free throws, Hunter did not miss a shot in the second half, going 5-for-5 from the field to finish with 14 points.

"His second half was key for us," Tony Bennett said of Hunter's play. "He attacked. De'Andre really did the things we needed, got us different kinds of baskets, whether it was a drive, got a couple of offensive rebounds, and really a very strong second half for sure."

Asked during the pre-championship press conference if his Final Four jitters were gone, Hunter didn't hesitate on his reply.

"I would say so, but I don't know what tomorrow is going to bring. There may be some nerves again, and I'm sure there will be, because it's the national championship game. There will be some nerves, we're going to have some jitters, but when it comes to the game, we are just going to play how we usually do."

\*\*\*

Fans and media alike wondered what was causing Hunter's scoring funk, and questioned if he was pressing.

Bennett said how impressed he was with his big guard's play in the second half against Auburn, and pointed out that even in the Elite Eight game against Purdue, Hunter had made two big free throws and a basket to seal the victory.

"He's always defending, and I just keep challenging him," Bennett told media during off-day interviews at the stadium. "I think he's just scratching the surface of what he's going to become."

The coach emphasized how intense postseason play was, how the physicality, the pace, everything magnifies in such settings.

"If he's missing shots, he puts a lot on himself," Bennett said. "We talked about it. 'Be free, man. Go after this. We need you. Be a player. If the shot's not going or whatever, impact the game in other ways.' That's kind of what we talked about, and I thought he took a step for sure in [the Auburn] game. He's hard on himself, but I know we're going to need it, obviously, tomorrow."

Bennett's words were prophetic.

\*\*\*

As clutch as Hunter's second-half performance was against the Tigers, it was a mere precursor of what was to come in the championship game against another red-hot team, Texas Tech, which had knocked off a former UVA nemesis, Michigan State, in the other semifinal.

Once again, Virginia's most dangerous player got off to a slow offensive start against the 31-6 Red Raiders. At the half, Hunter was 1-for-8 from the field, his lone basket coming at a key time on a drive to the hoop, knotting the game at 29-all with 90 seconds to play until the break.

Struggling on the offensive end, Hunter was still contributing with four rebounds, was 3-for-4 at the free throw line, and more importantly was slapping some wicked defense against Texas Tech's own projected lottery pick, Jarrett Culver. Hunter, both the ACC's and National Defensive Player of the Year, had locked up Culver, who had three points in the first half (all from the free throw line) and 0-for-6 from the field.

Still, UVA's chances of taking home the national championship trophy were slim without Hunter picking it up in the second half.

No one was more aware of that fact than Hunter.

"I knew my team needed me, and I knew I had to come out and be aggressive," he said.

Anyone with lingering doubts as to whether Hunter had the talent, ability, or determination to take over a game, were about to discover just how commanding he could be.

Hunter came out with guns blazing like in an old cowboy movie, turning U.S. Bank Stadium into his personal shooting gallery, gunning down the Texans with salvo after salvo, each a dagger into the Red Raiders' midsection.

Again, he attacked from the inside-out, earning two early free throws, then scoring from the paint to expand UVA's lead to 40-31 early on. He drilled a pair of impressive three-pointers in less than two minutes, sandwiched around a Jerome jumper. The big Cavalier guard continued his assault against one of the nation's best defenses as the game remained tight heading into the final minute of regulation.

Down 68-65 with 22 seconds to play, Virginia likely had one last opportunity to pull out another miracle finish, just as it did against Purdue in the Elite Eight and Auburn in the Final Four semifinal.

Texas Tech had scored the last seven points and had the momentum. But Virginia still had Hunter on its side, and that was enough.

With most of the 72,000 fans on their feet to watch the final seconds, Jerome brought the ball up court, flashed past his initial defender, drove into the lane, drawing Culver from the right side, leaving Hunter wide open in the right corner.

Jerome quickly read the situation and jetted a pass to Hunter, who launched a three-pointer directly in front of the Virginia bench.

Swish.

Twelve seconds remained on the clock with the score deadlocked at 68-all. Texas Tech would get one last shot, and everyone knew it would be coming from Culver, who banged a missed three off the front of the rim.

JON GOLDEN

JOHN MARKON

Hunter rebounded but lost the ball out of bounds, giving the Raiders one more second.

This time, it was Culver again from the corner, but UVA's Braxton Key, who had switched off to guard Tech's best scorer, blocked the shot, sending the game into overtime.

Virginia knew all about overtime, and dominated the extra period in an 85-77 runaway to the national title.

\*\*\*

When it was over, it was difficult for the Cavaliers to fully take in what they had just accomplished, the first basketball Natty in school history.

"It's unbelievable," Hunter said, surrounded by reporters in the Virginia locker room. "I just kept saying, 'There's no way we just won.' It's just amazing the way we won the last three games. Something I've dreamed about. I dreamed about this as a kid, to have a great game on the biggest stage in college basketball."

In that second half, talk about a takeover. Hunter made 7-of-8 field-goal attempts, hit all four shots he attempted from three-point range, was 4-for-5 at the free throw lane, pulled down five rebounds and scored 22 of his career-high 27 points, all after halftime.

After the game, Texas Tech coach Chris Beard was reminded that Hunter had only five points at the break and was asked if the Virginia star just found another gear or was just difficult to stop.

"Without watching the film yet, I would say twofold," Beard answered. "We did have some defensive lapses, but you've got to give him a lot of credit. They iso'd him, and he hit just a lot of tough shots. Matt Mooney is an All-Big 12 defensive player. We had Matt on him. We put Jarrett Culver's length on him a little bit.

"He's a pro. We could have scrambled at him and ran at him a little bit more, and that might be a coaching mistake, but we were dialed in. We knew who he was. He just hit a lot of tough shots."

\*\*\*

ACC coaches knew the past two seasons what a nightmare of a matchup Hunter was with his 6-foot-7 height and 7-foot-plus wingspan. He was a defensive stopper from Day One upon his arrival to Charlottesville.

He was unique for an 18-year-old who amazingly already in high school had a high basketball IQ, a keen understanding of the game, how to use screens, how to find shots coming off them, and taking advantage of opponents' weaknesses.

Miami coach Jim Larrañaga quickly identified just how difficult it was to defend the Cavaliers' star after facing him the past two years.

"De'Andre Hunter is one of those multi-dimensional players," Larrañaga said. "First of all, you've got to give him credit for his defense. Second of all, he starts at three (small forward) and can play on the perimeter, make a three-pointer, or put it on the ground and take a [defender] one-on-one.

"He can switch onto a four (power forward), which makes your defense better. Plus, he can handle the ball, he can utilize screens to get himself free, he can make the three, he can put the ball on the ground and create a shot for himself, which they do a lot, especially with him driving left. He can post up, he can turn and face from the post and jab and jab at you and make that little rare 12- to 15-footer. That's a real challenge, because it's not a great matchup for anyone trying to deal with him."

\*\*\*

Making it to the Final Four and getting a shot at the national title was something that lured Hunter back to Virginia for his third season. He could have been a first-round NBA pick after his redshirt freshman year, which would have essentially made him a one-and-done.

When he broke his wrist in the ACC Tournament in Brooklyn and was declared out for the NCAA's, it proved disastrous for Virginia. Without the versatile Hunter, the Cavaliers didn't have time to make the necessary adjustments, and despite being the nation's overall No. 1 seed, were stunned in the first round by No. 16 UMBC in a history-making moment.

Most argue that UVA should have won that game even without Hunter, but certainly his absence was felt in the humbling defeat.

Even though he watched that game from the bench, Hunter said he felt he had lost that game. Regardless, it served as motivation to come back another year and shoot for the moon.

"I knew we were going to have a great team and a chance to do something special," Hunter said after capturing the championship. "We did that tonight."

Asked if that winning moment was what destiny felt like, a huge smile came across Hunter's young face.

"It does," he said. "It felt like we had to win this game. No other team went through what we did throughout the offseason and most of this year. We battled through a lot of adversity, came through in the clutch, and we won two big games in the Final Four."

Hunter had delivered in the biggest moments in Virginia basketball history. He knew critics were wondering if he could do so, heard the doubters question whether he was in over his head, whether his offense was good enough for the next level.

"What other people say doesn't really matter to me," Hunter said after. "I'm my biggest critic. I know I wasn't playing well. I knew I was going to have to have a big game."

Because it was the last game of the season, Hunter was determined to go out blazing. He decided that he was going to be super aggressive no matter what.

No matter how many shots he missed, he was going to keep shooting. That's exactly what he did, and when the shots started falling, it greatly enhanced UVA's chances of bringing home the trophy.

His battle versus Culver was a classic matchup. He wanted to be aggressive on both ends of the floor, and admitted afterward: "I honestly wanted to show I was a better player."

The Red Raiders' star scorer finished with 15 points, but was 5-for-22 shooting overall, 0-for-6 from the arc, and had a plus-minus rating of minus-3 for the game, compared to Hunter's rating of plus-8.

\*\*\*

We had all seen how Hunter had taken over games, just like he did in the

JON GOLDEN

NCAA first round against inspired Gardner-Webb, and like he did in Louisville earlier in the season after the Cavaliers survived a staggering first-half, three-point barrage by the Cardinals.

In that game, Hunter had sat most of the first half on the bench after getting two personal fouls. Bennett's rule is that if you get two fouls in the first half, you sit the remainder of the half. Meanwhile, Louisville was shooting lights out and led UVA, 37-27, at halftime.

"That's super frustrating, one of the worst feelings, because you know you're going to have to sit for the rest of the half and can't help your team," said Jerome, who has experienced that same frustration. "I know what Dre was going through. When he came out for the second half, he looked a little mad."

Hunter unleashed that fury on Louisville, and the Cardinals didn't know what had hit 'em.

CHRIS GRAHAM

In what Bennett described as a special performance, Hunter scored a then-career-high 26 points (only surpassed in the national championship game). Nineteen of those points came in the second half as UVA came back to win, 64-52.

Hunter also devastated Louisville on the defensive end of the floor, shutting down Cardinals' star Jordan Nwora, holding him to five points (2-for-9) after the break. Meanwhile, Hunter didn't miss a shot in the second half, going 6-for-6 overall and 5-for-5 at the line.

"Look at his statline," Bennett pointed out after that effort. "He was so efficient, about as efficient as it gets."

As usual, Hunter, a man of few words, was modest about his feat.

"I just got a little mad," Hunter said. "I just want to be out there, so when I get a chance, I just want to be aggressive. I was getting it."

Even then, Bennett talked about how Hunter's game was growing before our very eyes.

"He's just continuing to evolve his game. You can see it. He's improving, playing at a high level. In practice, he shows signs of that, but to do it in games is a little different, when we need it, and there are other really good players on the floor. When he's on the floor, he's such a matchup problem."

\*\*\*

Hunter was somewhat accustomed to miracle finishes, dating back to the season before at Louisville when he capped off UVA's astonishing comeback, in which Virginia scored five points in nine-tenths of a second to win on his three-pointer at the buzzer.

It was only natural that when the NCAA Tournament started, regardless of the opponent, that it was going to be a special moment for Hunter, who was going to finally get a taste of the real postseason.

"This is the most I've ever been excited about a game," Hunter said of facing Gardner-Webb.

The underdogs surprised Virginia and led by as many as 14 points in the first half before Hunter led a comeback. Early in the second half, he slammed home a two-handed dunk, looked skyward and roared loudly, a rare reveal of passion by the Cavaliers' best player.

"Dre doesn't play with a lot of emotion, so when you see that from a guy who has been wanting to play in this tournament for two years now, it was great to see," said Guy.

Hunter went on to score 15 more in the second half, leaving the scars of last year's upset in the dust.

He finished with 23 points, and at the final media timeout of the game with 3:41 remaining, Hunter alone had outscored Gardner-Webb, 17-14, in the second half.

"Hunter was a monster for us to guard, and for most of the country to guard," said Gardner-Webb coach Tim Craft. "I think [defending Hunter] was difficult for everybody in the ACC this year for the most part, so it was going to be a difficult challenge for us."

\*\*\*

Game after game, NBA scouts and personnel directors followed Hunter from one venue to another. What they saw at times, must have been eye-popping stuff to them.

When it was all over, as the confetti had fallen in Minneapolis and the reality of it all still had not squarely sunken in, someone asked Hunter if there was a better story of redemption.

"I don't think so," Hunter grinned. "If you can find one, you can tell me."

## TY JEROME
# The heart, the soul of the champs

Ty Jerome will be remembered for his seemingly effortless, ridiculously deep, cold-blooded three-point daggers, his perfect no-look passes, his countless, fearless, running floaters amongst the trees, his quick hands on the defensive end and his overall burning desire to win.

During Virginia's championship run in Minneapolis, Tony Bennett revealed the recruiting story of the gritty New Yorker.

"When you see it, you know it — and I knew it," described Bennett of the uncanny ability and basketball smarts that the surprisingly unheralded point guard displayed when the UVA coach stumbled across him on a recruiting trip years back.

Bennett was in Pennsylvania to check out another player when Jerome's play first caught his eye.

"[Jerome] was playing in that game, and he wasn't near as big and all that," the coach recalled. "And I just kept saying, 'Man, he's really good,' but in my mind I'm like, 'No, no, he's not moving that well. I don't know. But man, he's really good.'"

There was just something special about this kid, and the coach kept tabs on Jerome. As time went on, Bennett got to see him play a few more times. Jerome kept making an impression, and as Bennett had done many other times, he went with his gut and decided to go after him.

"I told my staff, 'I'm locking in on that young man. There's something there. I think he's got a chance,'" Bennett said. "And I bulldogged him and followed him, and he kept making a believer out of me more and more."

\*\*\*

When Jerome arrived on Grounds, he didn't get a ton of playing time with senior star point guard London Perrantes, a 32-minutes-a-game fixture, running the point during the 2016-2017 season.

JOHN MARKON

Jerome, who averaged right around 14 minutes that season off the bench, absorbed and learned as much as he could from Perrantes, and was handed the keys at the end of London's storied Cavalier career.

Jerome took over as the team's main ball-handler to start his sophomore season, and he was more and more impressive as the season rolled on. No one will ever forget his shot in the closing seconds to seal the win against Duke, UVA's first victory at Cameron Indoor Stadium in more than two decades.

With all the success that Jerome and the 'Hoos accumulated during his sophomore season, the disappointment following the loss to UMBC that brought it all to an abrupt end was stunning for everyone involved.

However, Jerome was eager to turn the page, get back in the gym and begin the path to redemption.

JOHN MARKON

In the offseason, he attended former Wake Forest and NBA superstar Chris Paul's point guard camp, which annually brings the nation's top floor generals from all levels together for a few days of drills and competition. Several NBA guards were in attendance, and Jerome went toe to toe with the best the country had to offer.

"Any time that I have the opportunity to play against other great guards, other great players, and be around people like Chris Paul or all the other NBA guards that were there," Jerome said, "it's just such a great opportunity, because you get to learn, and you get to go at those guys, and that's what I love so much about basketball — you get to really compete. So, that was an amazing opportunity for me, I learned a lot, and I got to show what I can do in front of a lot of people."

He certainly opened some eyes with his play at the event, and said he already knew what he was capable of, but added that it was nice to show other great players what he could do on the floor.

Most of all, he was impressed by the work ethic and attention to detail exhibited by the professionals in attendance, who worked alongside the younger players and gave them pointers throughout the camp.

"I think the biggest thing that I took away from that camp was how focused those guys are, how focused Chris Paul was," Jerome said. "So, he would go at like 6 a.m. — we would start camp around 8 or 9 — and he would be there at 6, and he would work out first.

"And then," Jerome said, "even when he would work out, when we were at lunch or when we were watching film or whatever we were doing … he never once turned his head to the sideline to look around, he was so focused and so locked in on what he had to get done, and I think that's something that you don't really see at the college level, and definitely not as you go further down the line. A lot of people look left and right and worry about what's going on around them — he was so locked in, as were most of the pros there."

\*\*\*

It would be a few months before Jerome would declare for the 2019 NBA Draft, but there was some unfinished business to take care of first.

Virginia was ranked fifth in the country in the preseason AP Top 25, but was picked to finish third in the ACC behind Duke and UNC. Jerome knew how good this Cavalier team could be, and described what it would take to make the most of that returning talent and experience.

"I think we all know what our potential is," he said, "but a lot of teams have potential, and the biggest challenge is to try to maximize every bit of your potential that you can. That's everyone's biggest challenge coming into the year. I think we're working every day to try to do that."

Adding his summer camp experience, Jerome spent the remainder of the offseason fine-tuning his skillset, improving on his weaknesses, working on his leadership skills, and paving the way to a stellar redemption run.

"Ty is a natural leader," said Bennett. "He's very vocal. He'll demand — and I've even encouraged him and challenged him, 'Hey, sometimes, some guys, you've got to figure out what guys need. This guy might need a pat on the back, this guy might need to be pushed a little harder, and it's a delicate balance being a leader.'"

Jerome took on the challenge head-on, making it just as important to read his teammates' needs as spending time worrying about his own game.

"I'm gonna do whatever it takes to help this team win," said Jerome in early November, "so I think that's probably the biggest challenge for me right now, figuring out how I can talk to each guy on the team, and how to keep my patience throughout the course of a game, because that's when I have to completely take myself out of the equation. I can't worry about how I'm playing. I have to worry about how my teammate's feeling, or how my teammate's playing, how I can get other guys involved more."

With the addition of freshman point guard Kihei Clark, Jerome was often moved off the ball to the two-guard spot as Clark quickly adjusted to the role of the main ball-handler, which opened up more scoring opportunities for Jerome.

As a result, Jerome put up 20 points in the first two games of the season — he buried six trifectas in the opener against Towson after a slow start, and added six rebounds, seven assists and four steals in Game 2 against George Washington.

"I think [Jerome] was always pretty assertive, but I think we need that from him," said Bennett. "He's worked so hard on his game, and his outside shooting and his body, all those things, to get in the lane. So, he's played two really good games, and I think offensively he seems to be assertive with the ability to find guys, and when we got in foul trouble, I thought he looked a little more assertive on that."

Added Jerome: "We look good right now, but we know how far we still have to go."

Even when he wasn't filling it up scoring-wise, Jerome was still contributing in other ways.

He was held scoreless in the first half against Dayton in the Battle 4 Atlantis semifinals, but finished with 15 points (7-of-10 from the charity stripe). He added 11 points, four boards, five assists and three thefts in the championship game against Wisconsin, and was later named to the all-tournament team.

Against VCU, which turned out to be the worst shooting game of the season for the team, Virginia trailed by five with less than seven minutes left when Jerome got hot.

He hit two long triples, one from each side of the floor, in a matter of just over a minute — the latter came with an off-ball foul of Guy that resulted in a huge five-point sequence that propelled the team to victory.

Ten days later, following winter exam break, Jerome went off for 25, six and seven at South Carolina, shooting 9-of-15 from the floor, including rattling off 13 straight points in the first half. Three days after that against William & Mary, he hauled in a career-best 10 rebounds.

He set a new career high in the assist category while registering his first double-double with 14 points and 12 dimes in the blowout win against Virginia Tech at JPJ in January. It sparked a streak of seven straight games in which Jerome scored in double figures.

After emerging victorious in the first 16 games of the season and owning the nation's longest winning streak, the 'Hoos dropped a tough 72-70 decision at Duke on Jan. 19.

"We had that game. We lost it. We made mistakes that we can control," said Jerome.

He flirted with a triple-double — 13 points, nine rebounds and six assists — at Notre Dame before spraining his back in the overtime win at N.C. State, a game in which he posted a dozen points, six rebounds and six assists.

The injury kept Jerome out against Miami, ending an 88-

JON GOLDEN

game playing streak, but he still contributed in a different way. Before the game, Coach Bennett asked Jerome, who was sitting out the first game of his Cavalier career, to talk to his teammates throughout the contest about what he was seeing from the bench.

"One time, I came to the huddle, and Ty had something [drawn out] on the whiteboard," Bennett chuckled. "And I was going to say, 'Not that far.' But actually, I trust him that way."

Added Guy: "Ty did the same thing he always does as a leader. He pulled me and Dre aside a couple of times, and pulled other players aside, too, and had some one-on-one [discussions]. He's a tremendous leader, and he showed why he's a tremendous leader."

Clark stepped up his play without the services of Jerome, and the 'Hoos took care of the Hurricanes, and then had a week off to rest, get healthier and prepare for the rematch with Duke, and the biggest question heading in was the availability of Jerome.

He battled through the injury against the Blue Devils, getting the start and

JOHN MARKON

finishing with 16 points, but the Cavaliers couldn't keep up with Duke's better-than-usual three-point shooting (62 percent, about twice their season average).

"The medicine is starting to wear off a little bit, but I haven't thought about Carolina yet," Jerome said after the game, "I was just worried about [Duke]. I'll sleep, and then tomorrow see how I feel."

Less than 48 hours later, the 'Hoos were about to tip off at the Dean Dome against North Carolina, and Jerome was huge in the comeback win. He notched his second career double-double (15 points, 11 assists) to lead the charge over the Tar Heels, a defining win that would ultimately give UVA the head-to-head tiebreaker over UNC at season's end.

But Jerome and the Wahoos weren't done. He had 16 points in the season sweep in Blacksburg, and 19 soon after against Georgia Tech to clinch a double-bye in the ACC Tournament.

"That's a great accomplishment, and we're thankful for that," Jerome said. "You never want to take anything for granted. We worked really hard to [secure a top-four seed], so we're thankful for that, but we have such a long way to go, so much better to get. So, we just have to keep working."

Then, on the road against Syracuse in early March, Jerome turned the Carrier Dome into his own personal shooting gallery. He sank five long bombs — including one from just inside the big block 'S' at midcourt — in a three-point massacre of the Orange, and matched a single-game record with 14 assists to go along with four steals.

"They shot the ball as good as I've ever seen it shot," Jim Boeheim — who's been the Syracuse coach for decades — said of the Cavaliers' sharpshooting. "They didn't just make easy wide-open [threes]. They made some wide-open threes, but they made about six of them from six, seven feet behind the line. There aren't that many teams, if any, that can make those kinds of shots."

Jerome capped off the regular season with a game-high 24 points in the finale against Louisville, which clinched another ACC crown.

In the ACC Tournament quarterfinal matchup with NC State, Jerome scored just two points on 1-of-11 shooting (0 for 6 from deep), but dished out 10 assists and nabbed four steals as the 'Hoos moved on.

He looked a little better in the loss to FSU, and later revealed that he had come down with a "really bad virus" heading into the tournament, and was ready to get back in the gym and get ready for the ultimate test.

\*\*\*

Jerome made every minute count in the NCAA Tournament.

After facing a double-digit deficit against No. 16 Gardner-Webb in the opening round, Jerome helped lift the Cavaliers with 13 points, six assists and three steals.

"We're nowhere near relaxed, nowhere near satisfied," said Jerome after Virginia eliminated Oklahoma the following round. "We're not even close to our end goal."

In the Sweet Sixteen game against Oregon in Louisville, Jerome finished with 13 points, six boards, six dimes and a pair of steals, and the 'Hoos were halfway there.

He scored 24 points, grabbed five rebounds, dished out seven assists and played all 45 minutes in the overtime barn-burner against Purdue, and was part of one of the most memorable plays in NCAA Tournament history.

Jerome drew iron (let the debate live on regarding whether or not it was on purpose) on his second free throw with time winding down in regulation, which led to a Mamadi Diakite tapout and eventual game-tying buzzer beater.

The 'Hoos prevailed in OT, and Jerome shared what he was thinking during those intense final moments.

"There was so much going through my mind. I didn't really miss [the second free throw] on purpose. I short-armed, and Mamadi did a good play by hitting it, and Kihei made the play of the century."

Jerome finished the national semifinal tilt with Auburn as UVA's scoring (21), rebounding (nine) and assist leader (six), nailing four triples. He set up the game-winning free throws and was again at the center of a pivotal sequence at the conclusion against the Tigers.

After Jerome found Guy in the corner for a three to cut it to 61-60 with just seconds remaining, Auburn's Jared Harper then split a pair of free throws. Jerome got the rebound on the miss and quickly got fouled, as the Tigers had two fouls to give.

Jerome was advancing the ball upcourt with time running out, his Cavaliers trailing by two, when he dribbled the ball off of his heel trying to go behind his back, and picked it back up. Bryce Brown, who was then called for team foul No. 6 with 1.5 ticks left, was attempting to foul, and grabbed Jerome's jersey prior to him losing control of his dribble.

Afterwards, angry Auburn fans insisted that Jerome should have been whistled for a double-dribble, but there was a counter argument that the officials had missed Brown's foul first.

Play continued out of a timeout, and on the ensuing inbound, Jerome passed to Guy on the run, who was fouled behind the three-point line and went on to sink all three from the stripe to send the 'Hoos to the title game.

"Chaotic, man," Jerome said of the final sequence. "Just like the last game we had. You know, we always believe, and Kyle made a great cut and came up really clutch on making three free throws."

Jerome hit a momentum-shifting three-pointer at end of first half against Texas Tech to give Virginia a 32-29 edge. He came up big again in the closing seconds of regulation, driving and dishing to De'Andre Hunter for three to send it to OT.

Jerome sank two crucial free throws to give UVA a two-possession lead with 41.5 seconds left in the extra session, and then later sealed it with a long inbound pass to a wide-open Braxton Key, who slammed it home with 17 seconds to go, and the dream had become a reality.

JOHN MARKON

JOHN MARKON

Jerome easily could have been named Most Outstanding Player with his performance in the NCAA Tourney. He averaged 16.5 points, 5.2 rebounds, 6 assists and 1.5 steals in 39.5 minutes per contest in the tournament, committing just 10 turnovers in six games, and shot 41 percent from beyond the arc in the Big Dance.

\*\*\*

During the Scott Stadium celebration, fans chanted, "One more year," but Jerome entered into the NBA Draft two days later, and plans to turn pro in the summer.

Bennett knew it when he saw it, and the UVA faithful saw it for three unforgettable years of an amazing journey.

Ty Jerome's heart, his unwavering determination and his love for the game will never be forgotten by the folks in Charlottesville or Wahoos around the globe.

## MAMADI DIAKITE
# Key contributor to title team

For three years, we all waited patiently for Mamadi Diakite's switch to come on, for something to click, for him to "get" basketball.

When it finally happened, it was lights out for Virginia's opponents.

Diakite was a soccer player growing up in Conakry, Guinea, an African nation. Once introduced to basketball, there was no question that it made more sense to pursue that sport considering his 6-foot-9 frame.

When he arrived to Blue Ridge School, not far from Charlottesville, UVA coaches began to take notice.

JON GOLDEN

As Diakite helped Blue Ridge to a state championship in 2015, it was inescapable that his athleticism was off the charts. His knowledge of the game wasn't. Still there were reasons to be excited about his recruitment to Tony Bennett's program.

A redshirt year gave him extra time to become acclimated to college ball and develop his body for the rigors of ACC play.

When he began playing as a reserve forward in 2016-2017, there was no hiding his athletic ability. A high jump champion in high school, there was plenty of spring in his legs, which helped him finish 10th in the ACC in

JOHN MARKON

blocked shots (three each against Virginia Tech and North Carolina) in 32 appearances and one start.

The next season, as a redshirt sophomore, Diakite played in 34 games and showed flashes of brilliance. Because of his leaping ability, he was dangerous offensively if he had a clear path to the basket, dunking the ball with ease and often in dramatic fashion en route to a 57.7 field goal percentage.

Still, with all that often mind-blowing physical prowess, he sometimes appeared lost.

He admitted on more than one occasion that he was still trying to absorb the intricacies of the game. On the job training.

"Sometimes, when the coaches tell me to do something, I don't understand what it is they want me to do," Diakite confessed.

Athletically, he was superior to almost anyone he faced.

"Even in some of my years in the NBA, it was very rare that you came across an athlete like him," said Mike Curtis, Virginia's strength and conditioning coach, who returned to his alma mater after working in the big leagues for a number of years. "He possesses some gifts that you don't see very often.

"In terms of explosiveness, in springiness, mobility, all of those things are at a very high level. We haven't had an athlete at Virginia (during the Tony Bennett decade) that has had the genetic gifts that Mamadi has. That's God-given stuff that all of us wish we had at some point, but only a few get."

\*\*\*

If that light switch would only turn on: and with it, a clearer understanding of the game, its nuances, his assignments, his footwork, his knowledge. Diakite said late in his sophomore season that he felt he was edging closer to that day of clarity. In October of 2018, the redshirt junior said that things had clicked for him, and he was ready to show the world.

He wasn't kidding.

At UVA's media day, Bennett declared Diakite as the team's "X-Factor," a player who could make the difference between winning close games, or turn a good season into a great one. Oh, there were other "X's" on the team, such as Alabama transfer Braxton Key and freshman point guard Kihei Clark, both of whom would make major contributions. Diakite, though, was ready for a breakout year.

There were moments during the regular season, where Diakite wowed sold-out John Paul Jones Arena, and even impressed opposing fans at road venues, as he played in all 30 games, starting 17 times. Along the way he shot 53.7 percent, including 41.7 percent from three-point range, reaching double figures eight times.

Wahoo fans hadn't seen such a shot blocker since the days of Ralph Sampson, as Diakite put together a 20-game streak of at least one block. He finished the regular season ranked 10th in the ACC in swats.

He also posted good offensive numbers, scoring 18 points against Coppin State and Boston College, scoring UVA's first seven points of the game against Wake Forest before finishing with 11, posting 10 points and a then-career-high four blocks to go with seven rebounds at Notre Dame.

He registered 14 points and three blocks at Louisville in the Cavaliers' second-half comeback win. In another impressive road win shortly afterward, the big forward recorded nine points, five rebounds, and four blocked shots in a Wahoo blowout at Syracuse.

\*\*\*

It was at Louisville where the free-spirited Diakite showed up with tinted blonde hair, a la former NBA head-turner Dennis Rodman.

His girlfriend influenced him to make the bold change, a new look that earned him plenty of good-natured ribbing by his teammates, some odd double-takes by his coaches, and his mother's disapproving concern via telephone conversations back in Guinea.

Aminata Kaba wasn't exactly crazy about her son's new look, even after he told her it was the rage in America (a slight fib in attempting to ease her pain).

"Before the [Louisville] game, I made sure I talked to my parents," he said. "The first words my mother said was, 'What have you done to yourself?' after I had sent her a picture. I told her that's the new look in America, and she said, 'OK, no more.'"

His parents, Aminata and father Aboubacar Sidki Diakite, both doctors, usually catch replays of their son's games because of the time difference.

Reactions varied in Charlottesville.

"My teammates, I just walked in, and wow, they started videotaping me," Diakite chuckled. "Coach Bennett? He liked it. At first, I thought he would say something about it, and so I was ready to go back and get another haircut. But it seemed he liked it."

The new look seemed to give Diakite energy down the home stretch of the regular season. However, something changed as soon as the Cavaliers entered the postseason at the ACC Tournament in Charlotte.

Diakite was almost non-existent in those two games, a win over N.C. State in the quarters and a semifinals loss and tournament exit against a physical Florida State team. The Virginia leaper played only seven minutes against the Wolfpack and was pulled after a 13-minute appearance in the first half versus the Seminoles.

In those two combined games, he was 2-of-7 from the field for five points, had no rebounds, no blocks, and was dominated by FSU's lengthy roster.

In the week between defending ACC champion Virginia's exit from Charlotte to the NCAA Tournament opener in Columbia against Gardner-Webb, Diakite did a lot of soul-searching. He had a little help in the form of Dr. Tom Perrin, a former UVA assistant basketball coach under Terry Holland and Jeff Jones, who had gone on to become a successful sports psychologist/consultant for the U.S. Olympic soccer team, several NBA teams, and businesses around the country.

Perrin had previously worked with UVA star Malcolm Brogdon, then was asked by Bennett to work with De'Andre Hunter, then Diakite and Jay Huff. In the case of the latter three, it was about confidence-building and learning how to better and more efficiently improve their mental outlook on the game.

Perrin doesn't coddle players, but has frank, one-on-one conversations about accountability and expectations.

"Mamadi and I had some pretty direct chats," Perrin said. "I talked to him the day before the team left for Columbia. We had a hard conversation right after the Florida State game.

"I asked him, 'Where were you on Friday night against Florida State?'" Perrin shared. "It was pretty direct."

Diakite later admitted that he was in a bad place the day of the FSU loss. The Seminoles were physical, and Diakite did not respond. The fact that he met with Perrin, as he and Huff would do individually over the course of the season, was a huge factor in getting Diakite turned back in the right direction.

"Tom has helped me through a lot of ups and downs," Diakite said. "Every time something is not going right for me, I'll call him, or he texts me to see if I want to meet."

The session prior to UVA's trip to the NCAA postseason was an important one.

"We talked, and [Perrin] told me how much energy I have to bring," Diakite said. "I don't have to be too high. A 10 is too high. That's way too much energy. I can feel very loose and focused at about six. I need to be somewhere around a seven-and-a-half to eight for a big game."

\*\*\*

Whatever the two discussed paid huge dividends the remainder of the season, through six NCAA Tournament games and the Final Four championship. Diakite was a different player after that FSU loss, and that was a good thing for the Cavaliers. It was also a great thing for Diakite, who would go on to become an overnight celebrity in the college basketball world in the Elite Eight game.

But first, Diakite had to prove to Bennett that he was worthy of more playing time. Heading into UVA's first-round game against Gardner-Webb, Bennett knew his team had a distinct size advantage, and that Diakite could play a key role if he could deliver. He actually went to Bennett and apologized for his play in the ACC Tournament and promised his coach that given another chance, he wouldn't disappoint.

Bennett thought about starting Diakite in that NCAA opener for the Cavaliers, but could he risk his big man turning in another lackluster, sub-par performance? He decided it would be better to bring Diakite in off the bench, and this time his leaper was back to his old self, with an impressive 17-point performance. The athletic forward was 8-of-10 from the field, including some flashy dunks, and pulled down a then-career-high nine rebounds in 26 minutes, as UVA fought off a sluggish start and advanced to a second-round matchup against a high-scoring Oklahoma team.

Again, Bennett had a decision to make about whether or not to start Diakite against a mobile Sooners' squad. It was clear that regular starting big man Jack Salt might be less effective against Oklahoma's quickness in the post. But could Bennett trust Diakite?

The Virginia coach debated with himself for hours on who to go with, and settled on Diakite, but not without challenging him to remain focused.

Bennett went with his gut and started Diakite and the big man delivered. He scored 14 points, connected on 7-of-9 field goal attempts, again tying his high in rebounds with nine, in addition to blocking three shots and altering others with his jumping ability and impressive wingspan.

From that point onward, Bennett believed he could trust Diakite, particularly against teams that would be very mobile.

All along the way, the big African was also getting daily input from UVA associate head coach Jason Williford, who works with the Cavalier big men. Diakite praised Williford for helping him grow on the court, while Perrin helped him off it.

Williford has been gradually bringing Diakite along since the beginning and is proud of his improvement.

"Mamadi's ability to block shots and defend has been tremendous,"

JOHN MARKON

Williford said. "Whatever scoring punch he gives us is a plus. I think he's playing with a tremendous amount of confidence.

"Things have just clicked for Mamadi," Williford continued. "He has to focus, he has to stay there, but the game has slowed down for him. That's what happens when you become a veteran."

Against a talented and lengthy Oregon team, which boasted four starters all at 6-foot-9, Diakite's ability to move and defend would be critical. He more than held his own with seven points (3-for-7 shooting), two blocks and a new career-high 11 rebounds.

JOHN MARKON

"I was more aggressive on the boards and putting a lot of pressure on [Oregon]," he said. "Defensively, I wasn't allowing them to get a lot of rebounds over me. I was first fronting bodies, although sometimes some of the guards were very aggressive on the boards. It was hard to guard them. Every timeout, we're coming out with more energy. We're like lifting up each other, and telling each other we need to do it in order to win the game."

\*\*\*

Having survived the Quack Attack, it was on to face Purdue, which had knocked off Tennessee in a wild, high-scoring battle. Louisville's KFC Yum! Center, host of the South Region finals, was jam-packed with Boilermakers fans, almost like a home game for Purdue.

Little did Diakite suspect that his name, along with teammate Kihei Clark's, would go down in Wahoo history for the season-saving play they would make at the end of regulation in this Elite Eight contest.

There's a T-shirt circulating around Wahoo Nation emblazoned with this text on the front: "The Tip, The Pass, The Shot – The Play." Dozens of people have attempted to capture those fleeting seconds with a slogan of some kind, but nothing has managed to appropriately describe what happened.

Virginia trailed Purdue, 70-67 with 5.9 seconds to play, when Ty Jerome was fouled and sent to the line for a one-and-one. Jerome made the first free throw. Meanwhile, Kyle Guy signaled to Diakite to tap the ball back out to half-court if Jerome missed the second.

True to script, Jerome missed, and Diakite slapped the ball, but deeper into the backcourt than he intended. Clark doggedly chased down the loose ball, took a dribble, instantaneously sizing up the floor, and saw that both Jerome and Guy were covered. He spotted Diakite wide open to the right of the lane and whipped a perfect one-handed pass to him, shoulder-high, so that Diakite could catch and shoot.

Within a split second, Diakite released the jumper and swished it as the buzzer sounded. Virginia had incredibly tied the score and sent the game into overtime, where the Cavaliers would go on to win, 80-75, sending UVA to its first Final Four since 1984.

When the shot slipped through the silk, Diakite had this stunned look on his face as Salt ran up and bear-hugged him in front of the excited Virginia bench.

Later, in the press conference, Diakite was asked to take everyone through that last shot in regulation. He was still numb.

"I don't know," Diakite said. "It happened. I took it, and it went in. I was happy and ready for the next five minutes. I don't know how to talk about it. It was unbelievable. I don't know."

Bennett added a little more defining narrative to the play.

"Ty was clapping [for Clark to pass him the ball on the play]. I was like, 'Throw it to Ty, we'll get one up there.' Mamadi, to catch it and get it off that quick, so improbable."

Once again, Diakite was clutch. He made 6-of-11 shots attempted for 14 points, including two of the biggest points in Cavalier history. He blocked four shots and added seven rebounds.

He also became somewhat of a national media darling and a hero back home in Guinea.

"A couple of teammates told me it's all over Africa now," Diakite said in an interview session at Minneapolis two days before the Final Four games began. "The news is talking about it, and I'm up there. My cousins told me that if I go back home right now the whole population would come welcome me home. And here in the U.S., everywhere I go, people want to take pictures with me. I just saw Grant Hill, and he told me how proud he was."

ZACH PERELES

Some people related Diakite and Hill, who had made the famous inbound pass to Christian Laettner in Duke's miraculous last-second win over Kentucky in 1992.

Bennett got a kick out of Diakite's instant celebrity status.

"I don't watch a lot of TV, but I'm sure he's the toast of the town in so many ways," the UVA coach said. "His shot was amazing. That shot will go down, the pass and the shot, in Virginia basketball history. From the start of the year, I said he's an X-factor for us, and the way he's played all tournament has been significant."

\*\*\*

While media following the team all season was more than aware of Diakite's background and his change in hair color, he became a curiosity to national media. Bennett was quizzed about that, too.

"As far as his hair, if it's like Samson (the Bible character), and he's got to do it, so be it. It looks better in person than on TV. I see it when I watch video."

Bennett was also asked about Diakite's personality, which is of an outgoing nature, full of life, great sense of humor.

"If you're around him, he's got incredible joy," Bennett said. "He's got an infectious personality. He's great that way. I couldn't be happier for him. I've told him and the guys to be thankful, be humble, but you'd better have an edge to play well against Auburn on Saturday."

Diakite continued his solid play against the red-hot Tigers, with a new career-high in blocked shots with five, to go along with six rebounds. His role took on more of a defensive focus in this game (he only took four shots and scored one bucket), but that was what was required to knock off Auburn and advance to the national championship.

Defense and rebounding would also be his focus against Texas Tech in the title game. He delivered with seven rebounds, two blocks and nine points to help the Cavaliers stake claim to the program's first ever national championship.

Talk about a turnaround from those two performances in the ACC Tournament to the six-game NCAA stretch. Over that six-victory span, Diakite made 60 percent of his field goal attempts (27-for-45), averaged 10.5 points per game, grabbed 49 rebounds (8.2 per game) and blocked 16 shots (2.7 per game).

When the Cavaliers stepped up on the podium in Minneapolis to be presented the national championship trophy, Diakite grabbed hold and never let go for at least the next week or so.

Every time he was pictured, the trophy was in his grasp.

He told media that he might even sleep with the hardware because he didn't want to let it out of his sight. Asked about his constant contact with the trophy at the national championship celebration at Scott Stadium the following Saturday, Diakite said that Salt had assigned him the duty of protecting the prize, and jokingly said that if Salt told him to do it, he was going to fulfill those wishes.

As of this writing in late April, Diakite was among the four Virginia players that declared their intentions to enter the NBA Draft, along with Hunter, Jerome and Guy. Those three said they were not returning. Diakite left that door open.

Cavalier fans are hoping he walks through it at John Paul Jones Arena in the very near future.

JON GOLDEN

# JACK SALT
## 'Big Kiwi' caps storied career

Jack Matthew Cooper Salt was a little-known player from New Zealand that Tony Bennett came across on the recruiting trail, saw something in and took a chance on.

Little did anyone suspect that Salt would become the winningest player in UVA history.

Salt, Virginia's lone senior on the 2018-2019 national championship team, accumulated a program-record 118 victories during his Cavalier career, more than any other player to ever don the orange and blue.

He's been referred to as "The Auckland Wall" and "The Big Kiwi," and you did not want to be chasing another Cavalier at full speed and blindly be on the wrong end of one of his bone-jarring screens. Teammate Ty Jerome described how he did his best to avoid them at all costs in scrimmages.

"He sets real hard screens every day in practice. Everyone knows where Jack is when you're on defense," Jerome said. "I make sure to go way around Jack.

"He absolutely doesn't back down from anything. … He sets great screens for you, and he does absolutely anything to win."

\*\*\*

Salt's a humble guy. He's not one for the headlines, the cameras, the social media. He is quiet, sticks to himself, and for more than four years dedicated himself to the success of Virginia basketball.

"I try to block myself off from all that stuff, praise or negativity," Salt said. "I just focus on the locker room."

The big man battled through back issues in his final season on Grounds, which limited his minutes-per-game average from 19.8 as a junior to 16.6, but every time he stepped on the court, you knew he was going to give it everything he had.

No other Salt performance was more memorable than against N.C. State in his final ACC Tournament. After not scoring in five straight contests to conclude the regular season, Salt had an eye-popping afternoon against the Wolfpack at the Spectrum Center in Charlotte.

He scored 15 of his career-high 18 points after halftime, helping the 'Hoos outscore State by 22 in the second half and advance to the conference semifinals.

Salt made seven of his eight field-goal attempts on the day, including an early jam that marked his first made bucket in seven games.

Afterwards, Kyle Guy, who had just lit up the 'Pack for 29 points himself, suggested that members of the media "should be interviewing [Jack], not me," Guy said. "He was the player of the game."

The first-half dunk must've opened Pandora's Box for the New Zealander, who became an offensive force that particular Thursday afternoon.

"We were struggling a little bit the first half, and I was just trying to do my part to help the team," Salt said. "I felt like I wasn't going up strong in the first half. I had two takes that were really weak. I wanted to improve in the second half."

He was even whistled for a technical for hanging on the rim a few seconds too long after a soaring, emphatic flush that drew a roar from the Wahoo fans in attendance. Salt explained the situation in the postgame press conference.

"I haven't jumped that far and dunked in a while," he explained, "and so I had to hold onto the rim, or else I would have fell on my head."

He went on to complete three — you read that correctly, three — old-fashioned, three-point plays in the second half alone (within a 12-minute span), finishing the game 4-of-5 from the charity stripe en route to his record outing.

"When he was hitting those, I knew it was going to be a good day," said teammate De'Andre Hunter.

As UVA fans know, Salt was never exactly a dependable free-throw shooter, owning a career percentage of 46 percent, but it was just his day.

"I didn't know if it was real," joked Jerome.

Prior to the tournament, Salt had adjusted his free-throw technique. Due to a lot of heavy weightlifting as a teen, he had damaged a shoulder, which had negatively affected his shooting touch on foul shots.

Bennett said, "I'll take 18 points from Jack Salt anytime."

\*\*\*

Although he may not have been much of a scoring threat altogether, he had his moments, but Salt will be remembered as an outstanding defensive player and an intimidating physical presence — although that wasn't always necessarily the case.

When he first arrived in Charlottesville in 2014, Salt took a much-needed redshirt year to bulk up and get adjusted to ACC basketball, and added 15 pounds of muscle by the time the next season rolled around.

Salt averaged just under seven minutes a game as a redshirt freshman during the 2015-2016 season. Over his next two campaigns, he started every game, averaging close to 20 minutes per contest, and he became a fixture in Bennett's starting five, building a reputation as a stingy rim protector and solid rebounder who could set a mean screen to free up space for his teammates to get open looks.

"We've got great shooters," he said. "If I get them open, they're probably going to get a bucket, so that's what I'm thinking when I set a screen. If I get a guy wide open, he's going to hopefully have an open shot and a great opportunity of making it, so that's my mentality for setting screens."

JON GOLDEN

Salt's certainly been known to lay out an opponent or two over the years, as Jerome pointed out when asked if his screens are ones that players don't ever forget.

"Oh, for sure," said Jerome. "Do you guys remember that N.C. State game [in 2017-2018]? He set a screen, and the dude was — he might've had to have been subbed out, and it was a legal screen, too."

That "dude" was the Wolfpack's Lavar Batts Jr., who made the mistake of tightly guarding Jerome in the backcourt without keeping his head on a swivel. Salt set a nasty screen that flattened him like a pancake, which led to a wide-open Devon Hall three-pointer on the other end.

JON GOLDEN

Along with the departure of Hall, losing Isaiah Wilkins to graduation after the 2017-2018 campaign left somewhat of a void on the team in terms of vocal leadership, but Salt stepped up and embraced that new role.

"Isaiah was a guy I looked up to, and (I) tried to learn as much as I could from him," Salt said.

Salt spent his final season passing on that knowledge to his teammates, and Bennett knew he could be one of the guys who would help lead by example on and off the court, and "not let that leadership slide," as he put it.

Even despite the limited playing time as a senior, Salt could always be seen encouraging his teammates from the sideline.

"I think Jack's voice and his heart and mind for it will be a real important piece for our defense," Bennett said in the preseason.

\*\*\*

A stint with the New Zealand national team in the summer of 2018 was a dream come true for Salt, who helped his country advance in a FIBA World Cup qualifying event.

"It was a huge honor representing my country," Salt said. "I was happy they selected me for trials, and that they picked me for the team. Playing in games that helped us qualify for the World Cup and get two wins was awesome. I'm excited for the next opportunity to play for my country."

Salt got the chance to play alongside some of his childhood idols in the process, a moment that he will always cherish.

"To be able to go out and play with grown men who are professionals, just to see how they deal with certain things, was huge, and some of the guys I looked up to when I used to play when I was younger, I got to play with, so that was an awesome experience for me."

Another cool experience for Salt and his UVA teammates was a summer-bonding whitewater rafting trip in West Virginia in the offseason.

"I love stuff like that. I'd never been before, but our manager thought it would be a good idea, and he swung it through a few other guys, and we said, yeah, we'd love to do it. So, we went out to West Virginia, and we had a great time."

The way Salt described the voyage through the rushing waters, he could have been talking about his senior season that was filled with ups and downs.

"We were out there for a while, it was like four hours, and the conditions weren't too rough. It was pretty relaxed. But there were a few patches where it got pretty intense. And that's just a good time, being out there with your team trying to navigate through these rapids, it was a really good experience, and I'm happy that our manager set that up for us."

As Salt pointed out, the team was already a close-knit bunch prior to the outing, but sharing it together, just as they had shared the unprecedented loss the previous season, helped them to grow even closer.

"We broke history for losing to a 16th seed, and that's not a good record to have," Salt admitted in the preseason. "It might motivate us individually to get more work in, but we're going to work regardless. [UMBC] played great and deserved the game, but I can't wait to play the first game of the new season."

✦✦✦

When that moment finally rolled around, Salt walked out with the opening lineup in each of the first two games before his longtime starting streak (70 games dating back to his freshman season) came to an end, as he sat out the third game with back stiffness against Coppin State.

He was back on the floor, albeit coming off the bench, in the first two games in the Bahamas before returning to the starting five in the championship of the Battle 4 Atlantis against one of the nation's top centers, Ethan Happ and Wisconsin, grabbing a then-season-high four offensive rebounds in the win over the Badgers.

Five days later, Salt bounced back strong with his only other double-digit scoring performance of the year, a 12-point, 7-rebound effort against Bruno

Fernando and Maryland in the team's first true road test. He was 5-for-6 from the floor in the second half, and helped limit the Terrapins' big duo of Fernando and Jalen Smith to just two baskets in the paint after halftime.

The elder statesman had previously endured all the playful razzing from his teammates about not registering a dunk on the season and having a then-career high of just 10 points.

As Guy stated afterwards, Salt "put us all to bed" with his outburst in College Park.

Salt went on to put up seven points and eight rebounds on the road against Clemson, and then again against Wake Forest, and he finished with seven points and nine rebounds against Miami.

Later on, Salt totaled just five points and five rebounds in 37 minutes over a three-game stretch against North Carolina, Notre Dame and Virginia Tech, and then went scoreless in 51 minutes over those final five contests prior to his career day against N.C. State.

"This year Jack has been asked to do something not many people are asked to do," said Jerome. "Going into a game, he doesn't know how many minutes he's going to get, or if he's even going to take one shot during the game, and his attitude never changes.

"He'll give 110 percent for us every single possession, and that's something you don't see in almost any other guy in the country," Jerome continued. "If you ask them to take 30 minutes one game and five minutes the next, I don't know any other guy in the nation that would

give you their all, and he does. He continues to lead every day. He continues to fight through back pain. He's just, he's a warrior, and I'll go to battle with him any day."

\*\*\*

Salt was celebrated in grand fashion before, during and after the regular-season finale, his Senior Day game against Louisville, with his parents, Maria Anstis and Simon Salt, his sister, Sophie, and other family members in attendance.

"I was very happy to have all of my family here," Salt admitted after the game. "This is the most family I have had to a game, and to walk on the floor with my mom, dad and sister, it meant a lot to me.

"I came here as a first-year, and there were amazing players. There was Anthony Gill, Mike Tobey, Darion Atkins, Isaiah [Wilkins] was coming in with me. I was just amazed at the talent that was here, and I didn't think I was going to play. But over the years, I just worked hard and just tried to listen to the coaches and learn from the players, and I have loved my time here."

JOHN MARKON

Virginia was playing for a regular-season ACC championship and the top seed in the conference tournament that day, but for Jerome and the rest of the Wahoos, this one was all about Jack.

"More important [to send Salt off with a win]," Jerome said. "We talked about that before the game. We didn't talk about the title. We talked about sending him off the right way because of all that he has done for this program, all he has done for each of us, and who he is as a person."

The 'Hoos held on to sweep the Cardinals, pushing Salt's career record against the ACC rival to a perfect 9-0, and Salt was the last one to climb up the ladder and cut down the net to a huge ovation.

Salt started, was 3-for-3 from the floor, scored eight points and grabbed five boards in 18 minutes in the ACC semifinal loss to Florida State, then went on to play a combined 10 minutes over the Cavaliers' first three NCAA Tournament games.

"If Coach [Bennett] puts me out there, I'll be ready," Salt said. "It is always a matchup thing, whether or not he thinks I am best out there at the moment. I will be ready no matter what, and I look forward to the challenge."

Bennett called on Salt for one last challenge against Purdue, and the big man gave it his all one more time.

"It's funny, before the Purdue game, I mentioned to the team in our hotel when we did our walkthrough, I said, 'Here's a guy who's a fifth-year senior, who started and played a lot, and all of a sudden now his role has been reduced,'" said Bennett, "and I remember talking to [Salt] and he said, 'Coach, I just want to advance. Whatever you think is best. Yeah, it's hard not to play, but whatever is best for the team.'"

Salt finished with five points, eight rebounds, and a pair of steals in 34 important minutes against the Boilermakers as the 'Hoos survived in an overtime thriller and punched their ticket to the Final Four.

He totaled just 12 minutes in the two games in Minneapolis, but closed the book on his memorable Cavalier career as all players wish — as a champion.

\*\*\*

During the celebration a few days later in Charlottesville, Salt announced his future plans to continue playing professionally. He hopes to also represent New Zealand once again in the 2020 Olympic Games.

One thing is for sure — Salt will go down in UVA basketball history as a gentle giant who gave it his all each and every game and put everything on the line to help his team succeed.

"This has been amazing," said Salt of his time in Charlottesville. "I've had the opportunity to be a part of a great team, I've met some of my best friends for life being at this school, and thanks to Coach Bennett for letting me come here. I've had an amazing experience."

JON GOLDEN

# KIHEI CLARK
## Freshman pesters himself into important role

When Kihei Clark arrived in Charlottesville last summer, fans wondered if the diminutive point guard, standing 5-foot-9, would make much of an impact during his first year on the team.

Like most freshmen, the Californian had his peaks and valleys through the campaign as Virginia marched to the regular season ACC title.

Instead of hitting the "freshman wall," Clark flourished in the postseason and saved the Cavaliers from doom in the Elite Eight matchup against a strong Purdue team.

Legendary broadcaster Jim Nantz described Clark's game-saving – heck, season-saving – pass to Mamadi Diakite as the best assist he has witnessed in college basketball.

Nantz, who has called 29 Final Fours and countless other college contests, was of course giving his take on the final fateful regulation seconds of the victory over Purdue.

Dozens of fans and media have attempted to put a proper name on what some simply refer to as "The Play." That description seems bland for what Clark helped pull off as he notched his name into the annals of Cavalier basketball history.

No. 1 seed Virginia was facing elimination, trailing the Boilermakers 70-67 with 5.9 seconds remaining in regulation when Ty Jerome was fouled and sent to the free throw line for two shots.

Jerome made the first, cutting the deficit to two points.

What would he do? Make the second free throw, and then Virginia would foul Purdue in hopes of a miss? Miss intentionally, with the idea being that Virginia could grab the rebound and score to tie the game?

Jerome stood at the free throw stripe waiting for game officials to hand him the ball for the second attempt. Meanwhile, Diakite lined up on the right side of the lane, positioning himself for a possible rebound and stickback.

Kyle Guy and Clark situated themselves behind the free throw circle at the top of the key.

Over the thunderous partisan Purdue crowd in Louisville's KFC Yum! Center, Guy signaled to Diakite that if Jerome missed, he should try to tap the ball back out toward midcourt. Jerome missed off the front of the rim and Diakite did as instructed, slapping the ball deeper into the backcourt than planned.

With Virginia's hopes ticking away, Clark chased down the ball, ignored Jerome, who was calling for it, and instead spotted Diakite open on the right side of the lane. Clark lasered a perfect pass from the backcourt to Diakite – a la Tom Brady to Julian Edelman – the ball arriving shoulder-high for a perfect catch-and-shoot as the wide-open Diakite cooly sank the 12-foot, buzzer-beating jump shot to send the game into overtime.

The Cavaliers went on to defeat Purdue, 80-75, and advanced to their first Final Four since 1984.

While some focused on Diakite's shot, the wiser basketball fan realized that Diakite would not have had an opportunity to tie the game had it not been for the amazing poise by his freshman teammate.

Had Clark passed the ball below Diakite's waist and made him reach for the ball, Diakite would have been unable to beat the clock, and the basket would not have counted.

"I think it was the greatest assist, maybe ever," Nantz said in the week leading up to the Final Four. "What Kihei Clark did, to chase down that tap into the backcourt, I'm telling you that 99 percent of everybody who plays the game would have panicked and launched the ball before they got to midcourt. It would have been a half-court heave, and your chances are one in 500. This kid whipped that ball to the frontcourt (to an awaiting Diakite). Clark has tremendous quickness to get to that ball. It was a tremendous moment, and Mamadi made a great shot."

Clark's poise was atypical for a freshman. What was typical was his own humble description of saving UVA's season.

"I knew we didn't have much time, but tried to advance the ball," Clark said of the play. "So that's like get it to Mamadi. As soon as I caught [the ball] and was dribbling, I saw [Diakite] right away."

After helping send the game into overtime and eliminating Purdue, despite Carsen Edwards' eye-popping, 42-point performance, Clark joined his teammates in ascending the first ladder of the postseason, clipping down the South Regional championship net.

"That was an amazing feeling, amazing feeling to get the win," Clark said. "I'm at a loss for words, but it feels great."

\*\*\*

JON GOLDEN

Only a few weeks before, the young point guard wasn't feeling so amazing. His game had slumped late in the season and critical fans didn't hold back on their own feelings.

Shouldn't be starting, some said. He's a liability because he was no threat to score. Opponents don't guard him because they know he won't shoot it. He's too small to defend taller shooters on the perimeter.

Those were the whispers Clark was hearing about his game, which probably didn't help his confidence in his attempt to climb out of the slump.

JOHN MARKON

Instead, he chose to stay away from social media and blocked out the noise. The only criticisms he regarded came from his coaches.

"I don't read that stuff," Clark said. "Some people tell me that people on Twitter talk about me, but I don't pay any attention to it. People are going to say what they're going to say, but I'm still going to play my game and put in as much work as possible."

Clark's mental toughness was one of the qualities that attracted Bennett to the West Coast guard. Clark won't back down regardless of the challenge, something the UVA coach admires in a player, regardless of size.

Bennett, who at 5-foot-11 was selected as the National Player of the Year Under Six-Feet as a senior at Green Bay, knows a little something about grit and determination.

Let pundits take their shots at Clark, or at Bennett for refusing to take the small guard out of the lineup.

They didn't see what Bennett recognized as valuable contributions to the team.

Not everyone had to score in double figures. That's what Guy, Hunter, and Jerome were for. Others had roles to play, and Clark played his well enough to satisfy Bennett.

"You can't concern yourself with the opinion of others," Bennett said amidst all the controversy. "Kihei has helped us. He guards the ball hard. He scraps, and he's made some good offensive plays for us, gives us a dimension that we haven't had in a long time."

Want to see Bennett get really excited, jump-off-the-bench-fist-pumping-high-fivin'-excited? Then watch for when a player ties up an opponent, forcing a turnover. Or dives on the floor for a loose ball. Or draws a charge.

Clark got those kinds of reactions from his head coach throughout the season. Anything on the scoring end was a bonus, a part of the game that Clark will surely improve upon as his career advances.

Guy, whose defense has improved over his three years in the program, but can't compare to Clark's, particularly in terms of quickness, readily will defend his young teammate from the harsh jabs of those who don't appreciate Clark's game.

"[Kihei] is picking up full court for 33 games now … you don't see me doing that," Guy said after UVA's lopsided win over Oklahoma in the second round of the tournament. "He's a selfless player. He doesn't care about stats. He does a lot of little things that help us win."

\*\*\*

In this case, size doesn't matter. During Bennett's career with the NBA's Charlotte Hornets, he was backup to former Wake Forest star Muggsy Bogues, who was a mere 5-foot-3. As Bennett would often point out during the season, he experienced firsthand how Bogues would "just get up into an opponent" and harass an opponent.

He saw the same ability in Clark.

Early on, Clark wasn't on Virginia's radar. Eventually Bennett received scouting reports from his staff about Clark, who had been spotted in AAU play between the Californian's junior and senior years. Bennett had heard that Clark decommitted from UC-Davis, and decided to give Davis' coach Jim Les a call so everything remained above board.

Les confirmed that Clark was legit, the real deal, and had indeed decommitted from his program. Les gave Bennett his blessing in pursuing the quicksilver guard, and the UVA coach wasted no time in landing his future point guard.

186 TEAM OF DESTINY

Clark had enjoyed a breakout summer of EYBL hoops and decided he could play at a higher level than UC-Davis could afford him.

"I wanted to see how high I could play," said Clark, who is from Woodland Hills, Calif. "I love competition, and I just wanted to prove to everybody that I could play basketball at the highest level. That's the reason I decided to go somewhere else."

Virginia was the early bird on the re-recruitment, but soon after the Cavaliers offered Clark, others followed. Gonzaga, UCLA, Utah, Georgia Tech and others became suitors, but they were all too late.

In Clark's mind, Virginia represented an opportunity to play in the ACC, the best basketball conference in the nation. Parlay that with playing for Bennett and his staff, and it quickly became a no-brainer.

He knew about Bennett playing point guard in the NBA, and the whole less-than-six-feet thing, so he figured he could learn from someone who had already been where he wanted to go.

One of the things Clark learned from the get-go with Bennett was taking care of the basketball. As long as Clark didn't turn it over and played smothering defense, that's all the coach wanted from the first-year.

"I value each possession," Clark said. "You can't turn the ball over a lot. Ty has helped me making the right reads on the offensive end, or how to play a guy on defense."

Clark learned from one of the best. Jerome was one of the national leaders in assist-to-turnover ratio, assists, and dogged reputation for not giving up the basketball.

As Jerome once picked the brain of his predecessor, London Perrantes, another tough-minded Californian, Clark absorbed all the knowledge he could from Jerome, the also tough-minded New Yorker, on how to play the position in Bennett's system.

"Kihei has grown so much from Day One," Jerome said. "I think his biggest asset to this team is his selflessness. He could care less how much he scores. He's just all about winning. He's all about the team. He'll give up his body for the team. Sometimes we have to tell him to be more aggressive, but he's just a great teammate and ultra-competitor."

\*\*\*

Jerome finished the season with 194 assists to 60 turnovers, playing major minutes all the way. Often, the Cavaliers would have three guards in the lineup with Jerome and Guy, joined by Clark, who despite less minutes, still finished the year with 93 assists to 37 turnovers.

His game really came on in the postseason, where he was the only player

JON GOLDEN

in the NCAA Tournament to shoot at least 41 percent from three-point range (minimum 15 attempts) and average four assists per game. Clark shot around 32 percent from beyond the arc for the season, and was a solid free throw shooter (81 percent).

In Bennett's offense, where sometimes guards are interchangeable, the play call often had more to do with things than anything else.

"We have certain plays where [Kihei] will bring the ball up ... he'll play the point guard position on certain plays that don't involve ball screens," Jerome said. "He'll ask me if I want the ball. He's just super selfless."

Clark knows that eventually in his career that it will become important for him to produce more offense, but that wasn't his focus as a freshman attempting to fit into a new system. He wanted to do anything he could to contribute to a team that was destined to have a good, if not great, season.

JON GOLDEN

"I don't score a lot of points (4.6 points per game)," Clark said. "I just try to get me team as many possessions as possible, whether it's taking a charge, getting a knock away, getting a steal. Anything I can do to help my team win. I know I don't have to score a lot, but I've got to shoot my open shot, because that's probably going to be one of the better looks we're going to get during any given possession, so I just have to shoot that shot with confidence."

Most of the season that was the case, except for a stretch after breaking his wrist against Morgan State on Dec. 3.

While most figured Clark would be out for some time, he didn't miss a single game. He played against VCU six days later with a cast on his left wrist and scored nine points, including a 7-for-7 performance at the free throw line. He had surgery the following day and used UVA's exam break to recover.

While he sported a cast on his wrist for a while, and it impacted his ability to shoot, Clark didn't have much trouble with his handle or passing, and especially his defense as he ended up with 20 starts in the 38-game season.

***

There were times during the season – particularly the postseason – when his best came out, like in the Gardner-Webb first round game of the NCAA Tournament. Facing another No. 16 seed, the Cavaliers staggered out of the gate and wobbled with confidence in the first half, unable to shake the memories of a year ago.

Clark, however, who had no such memories, dug deep and helped Virginia survive and advance with a statistical line that would raise eyebrows of the old coaches who appreciate such numbers.

In that game, Clark recorded three steals, four assists, one three-pointer, five rebounds, not to mention all of the tipped balls and chased down loose balls that he influenced.

Virginia may have fallen to another No. 16 seed that day in Columbia, S.C., had it not been for Clark's hustle.

Against Oregon in the Sweet Sixteen, the Ducks featured a lineup with four players at 6-foot-9, which definitely caused problems for UVA's smaller guards. Clark had to go head-to-head with the only sub-6-foot-9 Duck, 6-foot-3 Payton Pritchard, Oregon's leading scorer on the season.

Clark held Pritchard to 11 points on a 3-for-12 shooting night (only 1-for-6 from beyond the arc).

In that matchup, Pritchard's plus/minus for the evening was minus-4, while Clark's was the highest plus/minus of any player for either team with a plus-10. While Pritchard was handcuffed, Clark enjoyed a beautiful night, matching career highs in scoring (12 points), assists (six), three-pointers (three), and minutes (37) in UVA's 53-49 win over the Ducks.

"I'm so proud of Kihei," Jerome said of his understudy. "That's what I expect from him. He puts in the work. He's a confident kid. If I ever see him waver from that, I always tell him, 'Be who you are,' because he's a hell of a player."

\*\*\*

Those are the things that caught Bennett's eye and persuaded him to go after the cool kid from Cali.

"He's so competitive," Bennett said. "He's a winner. He's shown that.

"When I first watched Kihei, not a lot of people were. When you see [that something in a player] you know it," Bennett said. "He's got something in him."

It reminded the Virginia coach of a book or video from the past, something called "Don't Tell Me No."

"I watched [Bogues] heart and that perseverance. That's something that you have to have. I tried to identify with that. I understood that," Bennett said. "In these settings, to have that kind of mettle, and that kind of stuff, that's a good sign."

Clark doesn't hesitate when you ask him the focus of his responsibility. He likes to use the word "pester" to describe how he gets after opponents with his shadowing defensive ability.

He frustrated Virginia Tech's senior point guard Justin Robinson to the point that the Hokie was whistled for a technical foul after losing his cool and pushing the ball hard into Clark's stomach. Clark had definitely taken up residence inside Robinson's head, impacting the Tech veteran's shooting night (2-for-7 from the field, 1-for-5 from the arc).

"[Robinson] pushing me with the ball, that was a statement," Clark grinned. "I was just doing my job trying to guard him the best I could."

In fact, Clark does his job so well that it sometimes boils over in practice against his own teammates.

The story goes that Jerome was so annoyed with Clark's defense against him during one practice that in a heated moment Jerome threw the ball ... at Clark's head.

"Yeah," Clark confirmed with a canary-chomping-Cheshire cat grin. "No, I didn't manage to get out of the way."

Bennett loves to see his little guard with the low center of gravity and a pit-bull's mentality get under the skin of more heralded players.

That was never more evident than in the white-knuckled moments of the Purdue game, with everything on the line.

Boilermakers coach Matt Painter felt good about his team's chance to advance to the Final Four when he saw Diakite tap the ball so deep into the backcourt.

"That was a favorable tip-out," Painter said. "That's what you want. You want the ball to go away from their basket. A three can beat us. As a coach, when that happens, you're like get the basketball, guard the arc. The ball is so far out when it goes past half-court that you're not thinking that. We had the ball in the guy's hands that we wanted. Clark had the ball. With that being said, he made an unbelievable play to find Diakite.

"Play of the game," Painter said.

Jerome did Painter one better when asked about it during the postgame press conference.

"Kihei made the play of the century."

# BRAXTON KEY
## Virginia's Swiss army knife

The biggest question mark heading into Virginia's championship season was whether Alabama transfer forward Braxton Key would be eligible to play. Luckily for Wahoo Nation, the NCAA granted Key's request just weeks leading up to opening night against Towson.

He turned out to play a key role — pun intended — throughout the season, all the way through the magical run. It's hard to picture the overall success of the team without Key's vital contributions.

The nephew of Ralph Sampson, Key was recruited out of high school by UVA coach Tony Bennett, and the interest was mutual. Hailing originally from Charlotte, Key was twice named his division's state player of the

JON GOLDEN

year in Tennessee before transferring to Oak Hill Academy for his senior season in 2015-2016, leading the team to a 45-1 record, and was named Most Outstanding Player at the DICK'S National Championship.

So, how close did Key come to becoming a Wahoo from the get-go?

"Really close, I mean, they were in my top four," Key said of the possibility of committing to the Cavaliers. "I wasn't able to take a visit. I really wanted to, but [De'Andre Hunter] committed the week I was supposed to take a visit."

JON GOLDEN

Little did Key know at the time that he would go on to be teammates — and eventually celebrate a national title — with Hunter.

Key went up against Mamadi Diakite and Kyle Guy in the AAU circuit, and Guy did his best to bring Key aboard, but he chose to go down south and play for former pro Avery Johnson and the Crimson Tide.

"We both played in the Adidas Circuit growing up, so I mean, we've always had our little rivalry," Key said of his relationship with Guy, adding, "his team never beat mine."

He went on to reluctantly admit that Diakite's Team Loaded was the one that sent him out with a loss in his final AAU contest.

"Don't mention that to [Diakite], he talks about it enough," Key joked.

Key excelled as a freshman at 'Bama, earning SEC All-Freshman honors after posting team-highs of 12 points and 5.7 rebounds, while adding 2.5 assists per game.

He suffered a knee injury and sat out the first 10 games of his sophomore season, and eventually made the decision to transfer to UVA, requesting a hardship waiver so that he would be able to play for the 'Hoos immediately.

Key shared that even when he finally got a chance to visit Charlottesville and the University, he and coach Tony Bennett didn't talk too much about X's and O's.

"It was mainly just how he could help me grow as a person," revealed Key. "That's kind of what I was looking more forward to coming in here, and he's been a man of his word all the way throughout."

He explained that while some coaches are known to say whatever it takes to get a player's foot in the door, Bennett seemed extremely genuine. What's more, he had the confirmation of a few old friends, Guy and Diakite.

\*\*\*

Key made the decision to transfer to UVA, and there was a question as to what position he would end up playing if he was granted eligibility, small forward or power forward. Instead, he perfectly responded with a description of his Swiss-army-knife style of play.

"I think I'm a basketball player," he explained. "I don't really like to limit myself to one position or two. I can play whatever I need to, so if I need to play the point, sometimes I will do that. If I need to play the [center position] and battle down with guys like [Jack Salt], I'll do that. Whatever I need to do to help the team win."

Waiting on a decision from the NCAA in the offseason was tough, but Key stayed focused and ready in the event that he would be cleared.

"It was a long process, that's for sure," Key admitted during the team's media day, "but it's humbling. It's a blessing."

He also got a little help from his new teammates during the process.

"Kyle, Ty, Dre have been picking me up and saying, 'You may be able to play this year, you may not, but just if you are going to play, you might want to practice in case like you're gonna play.'"

That early chemistry with the rest of team — through practices and the annual intrasquad scrimmage — paid huge dividends throughout the course of the season.

Ironically enough, Key's final opponent as a member of the Crimson Tide was the same team the Cavaliers faced in their first preseason exhibition game, Villanova.

Of course, there was having to familiarize himself with Bennett's Pack-Line defense, which he admitted was challenging, but necessary.

"My system at Alabama was way different, just closing out, so kind of just getting your [footing] right and just forcing a certain way, and just making sure your two feet are in the pack," he said, explaining the learning curve. "So, it's been a big emphasis but it's been good. I've learned a lot so far, so I'm excited."

\*\*\*

Key got the start in the season opener against Towson, and everyone got a chance to see what this kid could do. When Salt and Diakite found themselves in early foul trouble, Key stepped up and provided a boost down low, as he did all year long.

"He was good on the glass, and he's versatile and brings physicality and awareness," Bennett said of Key's official debut, which essentially summarized the junior's entire campaign. "I thought that was important."

He finished his first game as a Wahoo with seven points and nine rebounds in 29 minutes — not too shabby, and a sign of things to come.

After making a good first impression, Key felt more comfortable in his new surroundings and talked about how sweet it was to play in front of a sold-out crowd night in and night out at John Paul Jones Arena.

"The fans get really hyped," he said. "I mean, I took a charge, and you'd think I dunked on somebody."

Key came up big down the stretch in UVA's first real test of the season against Middle Tennessee in the first round of the Battle 4 Atlantis, scoring 10 of his 13 points in the final 10 minutes while hauling in seven boards to help the 'Hoos advance in the Bahamas.

Fans will recall Key falling to the floor while pursuing an offensive rebound and bouncing up for a three-point play against the Blue Raiders.

In the ACC opener against Florida State, Key exploded for a season-high 20 points on 7-of-11 shooting (including a pair of threes).

"It felt great," Key said of his big night. "My teammates had confidence in me, and I had confidence in myself, so just whenever I had any open look, I just tried to be a little bit more aggressive today than normal, and the shots were falling for me today."

He only scored in double digits three other times all season, but led the team in the rebounding category and did all the little things that don't necessarily show up on the stat sheet, something he still had a tendency to fill up.

Key had nine points, nine rebounds, two assists and two blocks the next game at Boston College. He posted seven points, eight rebounds, three assists and two steals at Clemson, and registered eight points and eight boards at N.C. State. Although he only had four points in the rematch with Duke, he grabbed 10 rebounds (six offensive), while adding a pair of blocks and a pair of steals.

JOHN MARKON

\* \* \*

Key routinely did a lot of the dirty work in the interior on both ends of the floor — playing intense, lockdown defense against some of the ACC's best, boxing out, tipping and deflecting entry passes to create turnovers, diving for loose balls, and creating second-chance opportunities on the offensive glass.

He hit a bit of a slump in terms of perimeter shooting in the middle of the season, but busted out in the sweep of the Hokies in Blacksburg after countless shots put up in practice in the gym during the stretch.

After misfiring on his first two wide-open tries that night from beyond the arc, Key was encouraged by his teammates to keep shooting.

Key went on to nail a pair of dagger long balls to help put Tech away and silence the Cassell Coliseum crowd.

On the first, he displayed his elation, spreading his hands to the sky.

"I just said to myself, 'Finally.' You work so hard and not to get the results you want is frustrating," he said, "but you have to stay confident and stay with it."

Key kept contributing in every way possible and finished with nine points, five rebounds and two blocks against Louisville to help clinch the ACC regular-season title. In his first season as a Wahoo, he was already cutting down nets before the postseason began, and there were a few more to come.

\*\*\*

Key put up nine points and nine rebounds in the second-round win over Oklahoma. He and the Cavaliers were on to the Sweet Sixteen. After advancing through the South Region and trimming some more twine in Louisville, it was onto the ultimate goal, the final stop — Minneapolis.

It was none other than a familiar foe that Key would wind up facing in the next round on the biggest stage — the Auburn Tigers, the dreaded, bitter rival of his former school, Alabama.

"It's going to be funny seeing some guys I played against for two years," he said a day ahead of the Saturday showdown. "I got a lot of texts from my former ['Bama] teammates, former fans. They don't want to see Auburn make the championship, so we're going to do our best to make it happen."

Coach Bennett picked Key's brain once the matchup was revealed, gathering a few first-hand tips on how to go against the nation's deadliest three-point shooting team, which also led the country in steals.

"They thrive off of turnovers," Key said of the Tigers, "so we're just going to have to take care of the ball, rebound the ball well, and we're going to have to play one of our best games all year in order to beat them."

And the Cavaliers did just that, outlasting Auburn to advance to the final, and how sweet it was for Key, who stated that the old rivalry was still instilled in him.

But more importantly, there was just one more game to go for that "One Shining Moment" that all basketball players dream about, and Key played an important role in acquiring the crown.

Although Bennett "doesn't really tell you" prior to games, Key played 29 crucial minutes against Texas Tech in the title game, and made the most of every one of them.

"I kind of figured I'd play a lot," Key said. "I just knew with their physicality and how big they were, how strong they were, I might have a chance to play. I was thankful to play a little today, made my day."

And he, in turn, helped make the day of Virginia fans everywhere. He jumpstarted an early Wahoo run with a steal on one end and solid finish on the other.

He took a memorable tough charge on a fast break in the second half, dropped off a perfect bounce pass to Guy to put the 'Hoos up 65-61 with under two minutes, and matched his career-high with 10 boards — but most importantly came up with a gigantic defensive stop at the end of regulation.

After Hunter's three from in front of the UVA bench tied the game at 68-all with a dozen seconds left, the Red Raiders had one final crack at it on an inbounds pass with exactly one tick remaining.

JOHN MARKON

Key, who was originally guarding the inbounder, Matt Mooney, prior to a Tech timeout, later revealed during the championship celebration five days later at Scott Stadium how after an ensuing UVA 30-second stoppage, he got the defensive assignment against Jarrett Culver — Tech's go-to guy, leading scorer and Big 12 Player of the Year — in crunch time.

"Me and [Hunter] were gonna switch spots, and he was just like, 'No, bro. You've got it,'" said Key. "And I was like, 'Alright. You've been doing a great job on Culver all game, but I got you.' And then I was just trying not to foul, and then just made a big play for the team."

Culver had gotten off to a cold start — thanks in large part to the shutdown defensive play of Key and Hunter — but started to heat up when Chris Beard's Red Raiders made a late charge. He had just scored a go-ahead left-handed spin move off the glass on Hunter, the ACC Defensive Player of the Year, 34 seconds earlier, and everyone in the building knew he would be the one to take the big shot, the potential game-winner.

One slip-up defensively could have been costly, but Key delivered when it mattered most.

Mooney threw it in the near corner to Culver, who quickly released a shot, but Key was all over it. He smothered the attempt as the buzzer sounded, headed back to the bench to some well-deserved high fives, and the championship game went to overtime for just the eighth time, when the 'Hoos took over.

It was icing on the cake when Key capped the championship run with a wide-open, two-hand, fast-break jam off of a Jerome Hail-Mary pass, and then sealed it with a pair of free throws in the closing seconds (the Cavaliers were a perfect 12-for-12 from the line in the extra session).

\*\*\*

"There is no feeling," Key said in the victorious locker room, when asked to describe his emotions. "I'm just so blessed. For what we went through last year — and obviously I wasn't here so I wasn't a part of it — but just to bounce back from losing to a 16 seed.

"There's so much pressure in these games. … Every game, we were down, but we just found a way to fight, and I'm so proud of my team and what the guys were able to do this postseason."

For a guy who came in as a question mark, it was Key who put the final punctuation mark — and better yet, the exclamation point — on the most memorable season in Cavalier history.

In the end, he summed up exactly what it required for this special group to bring a trophy back to Charlottesville.

"We just have ultimate faith and ultimate confidence in one another and in ourselves," said Key. "We trust one another. The way we play, we don't think we can ever lose. With the way we play defense and the way we shoot the ball, it's so hard to count us out."

The 'Hoos proved that time and time again, and couldn't have done it without Key's contributions.

JON GOLDEN

# JAY HUFF
# Fan favorite steps up when called on

If there's anyone who made the most of his minutes for the Virginia basketball team in 2018-2019, it was redshirt sophomore center Jay Huff.

The UVA 7-footer has quickly become a fan favorite at John Paul Jones Arena — which he said was "flattering" — with his ability to shoot the trey just as well as he can throw down an alley-oop or slam one home from several feet away in one long stride.

A devout Christian, Huff came from a basketball family. Both of his parents played the sport in college — his mother, Kathy, at West Virginia; his father, Mike, at Pacific Lutheran. Growing up in the shadow of Duke University in Durham, N.C., many expected Huff, who naturally was a Blue Devil fan, to wind up playing for Mike Krzyzewski.

Huff and his family regularly attended games at Cameron Indoor Stadium, and the young Jay even traveled to Indianapolis in 2010 to see the Devils play in the Final Four.

When Huff was going through the recruiting process, Coach K showed interest, but never offered Huff a scholarship. When Tony Bennett did make an offer, Huff climbed aboard and signed with the Wahoos.

"I did really like UVA, and I like what they brought to the table, and what I felt like I could bring to the table [at UVA]" Huff said of his decision. "The place, the coaches, everything about it, seemed really cool. With Duke, it was more like that school that you grew up watching and all that, but I prayed about it a lot and eventually it was like, 'Alright. Nothing seems like it's gonna change my mind, and I want to go to UVA,' so I called Coach Bennett up … I converted very quickly, I like to say."

His father, Mike, who was also his high-school coach at Voyager Academy in Durham, admitted that he and the rest of the Huff family disposed of their Duke paraphernalia when Jay started attending UVA.

\*\*\*

Huff decided to sit out his first year in 2016-2017 and only played a dozen games as a redshirt freshman the following season, averaging 3.4 points in 8.8 minutes a game.

With the help of Virginia strength and conditioning coach (and former Wahoo) Mike Curtis, Huff put on 15 pounds between his first and second year, going from 215 pounds to 230. At one point he said he'd try to eat six meals a day, usually junk food, to help add weight to his lanky frame.

"Pizza and a lot of Cookout," Huff admitted of his old dietary habits, adding that he's trying to eat a little healthier these days.

When he finally hit the hardwood, Cavalier fans saw immediate flashes of Huff's capabilities in his official UVA debut against Austin Peay on Nov. 13, 2017, as he went 7-for-8 from the field (including a pair of three-pointers) and posted a career-high 16 points, while tying a JPJ record with five blocked shots in a career-best 24 minutes.

He didn't get many more opportunities to impress that first season, but stayed patient, kept working hard, and he knew in the back of his mind that his time would come.

Huff admittedly struggled with his lack of playing time over his freshman year and in the early part of his sophomore season, as he averaged just 8.8 minutes in just 12 games in his first season and only got a combined 24 minutes of action in the first two games in 2018, blowout wins against lesser non-conference opponents in Towson and George Washington.

"It was pretty difficult," he said. "I think patience was my biggest issue with that. I wouldn't say I was the most patient person before all that, so maybe that was just God's way of saying to just wait a little bit and be patient, and I'm sure that will help in other ways later on in life, as well."

He realized there was a certain area of his game he needed to keep improving on if he wanted to see more burn.

"I would say defense," Huff admitted. "I guess, more specifically, ball-screen stuff and getting back to my man. [Coach Bennett] says the word continuous a lot, and I was just learning to be more continuous. Learning from [Mamadi Diakite], learning from Jack [Salt], learning from [Isaiah Wilkins]."

In the third game against Coppin State, Salt was missing his first game since his redshirt freshman year, and Huff finally got another chance to show off his skills in a game situation, scoring nine points on 4-of-5 shooting in 16 minutes.

He didn't play much during the team's time in the Bahamas for the Battle 4 Atlantis, but blocked three shots in 15 minutes in early December against Morgan State, providing another glance at what he's capable of on the defensive end, much to the liking of Bennett.

"It was nice to see him bother shots and be active," Bennett said of Huff's performance. "He has good hands and skills offensively. [Morgan State] didn't

JON GOLDEN

set a lot of ball screens, but Jay just has to continue to work on his alertness and his activity. I thought he did a nice job. He had two good days of practice. We're going to need everybody, and I'm always looking for matchups for Jay out there, and I thought he did a good job and was alert.

"You could really see his length. Even if a guy beats him or beat someone else, he has the ability and the timing, with being 7-feet and being fairly quick off the floor, to bother a shot. So, rim protection is important, and he took a step in the right direction. Against a team that's a little different than some of the competition in our league, size-wise and some quickness, I thought he handled himself nicely on both ends of the floor."

Huff played just 13 minutes against Marshall on New Year's Eve, but posted a season-high 14 points to go along with a career-best eight rebounds.

In ACC play, Huff continued to step up his game in limited opportunities, coming away with an 11-point, seven-rebound performance that featured a sweet one-handed alley-oop finish from Kihei Clark, and did it in just 10 minutes at Clemson.

"I was so happy that Jay offensively came in and gave us that kind of lift. Even defensively, he wasn't great, but his length bothered [the Tigers] at times, so that was encouraging. … When he rolls on the rim, our guys know, 'Throw it up,' and he's going to go get it," said Bennett.

JOHN MARKON

Two games later, Huff finally realized a childhood dream — playing in front of the Cameron Crazies.

He only played seven-plus minutes, but scored on two beautiful dunks to temporarily quiet the Crazies. One was off a nice up-fake in close to get R.J. Barrett up in the air and out of the way. On the other, Huff used his three-point shooting threat, pumping at the arc to get Duke big man Marques Bolden to bite before soaring for an eye-popping, one-handed flush.

"Well, I'll be honest, I didn't think I was going to get it there," he later admitted. "I thought I was going to hit the front of the rim, fall on my butt and embarrass myself in front of a bunch of people."

Huff said his mother sent him a sweet picture of the dunk, and he admitted to watching the replay of it a couple times after the fact, too.

"I won't lie, I've watched it a few times," he laughed. "It's kinda fun to watch replays and stuff like that."

Huff said that although the Cavaliers came out on the wrong side at Cameron, he felt he played well, and gained a little added confidence going up against the most talked-about team in the land in his old backyard.

Three days later, back at JPJ against Wake Forest, Huff put up 12 points and two blocks in just 13 minutes.

That output was included during one stretch over five games of the early ACC slate, when Huff had scored 35 points in just 36 minutes of playing time. How's that for efficiency?

Against N.C. State, Huff caught a lob from Braxton Key and dunked it in, was fouled and completed the three-point play shortly after Wolfpack guard Markell Johnson nailed a triple to start overtime to give State its first lead of the game. The 'Hoos went on to escape with the win.

Huff scored eight points (including a pair of triples) in 14 minutes in the home rematch with Duke, then scored the go-ahead bucket and also came away with a huge steal late in the game two days later at UNC.

At Louisville, Huff made six of his eight shots (including a career-high three three-pointers), finishing with a dozen points, seven rebounds and two blocks in 17 minutes, then he led the team in rebounding (six) and steals (three) against Pittsburgh.

He played a season-high 18 minutes at Syracuse.

Huff talked about how he developed his unique skill set over time.

"Growing up, I didn't have a position, really," he pointed out. "I grew up doing all the ball-handling drills, all the shooting drills. My dad taught me all that, both at camps and just individually working with him, so he never coached me to play a specific position — probably because he didn't know I'd grow up to be seven feet.

"But I think it definitely helped."

\*\*\*

His playing time dwindled in the postseason, totaling just four minutes in the last four games, but his contributions throughout the 2018-2019 season will forever be remembered.

Shortly after four of his teammates had declared for the NBA Draft, Huff, known throughout the program for his sense of humor, took to social media to have a little fun.

"I would like to thank God, my family and my friends who have all supported me through this journey," read the post. "These past three years have been more than I ever dreamed it could be, and this team accomplished so much during my time here.

"With that being said, I would like to officially declare my intentions to STAY at the University of Virginia and finish out my time here. A HUGE

JOHN MARKON

congratulations to my teammates who have declared for the NBA Draft, and I wish you guys the best of luck. Thank you for everything you've done. We'll be here competing for another championship. ... Made y'all nervous, didn't I?"

With a full offseason to keep improving, along with the graduation of Salt and possible departure of Diakite, Huff is all but assured more minutes in 2019-2020.

So, now we know that Huff will, indeed, be back for at least one more season. Maybe it's time for a new moniker?

"There's so many nicknames," said Huff, shuffling through his memory for some of the best. "The Hoo-nicorn, The Huffington Post, The Huffington Posterizer, Hufflepuff, Huff the Magic Dragon, Huff Daddy ... there's so many of them. There's more, I can't think of all of them right now."

He said he prefers one in particular you've heard before — with a little bit of a variation — that unfortunately, he says, didn't exactly stick: "Dr. Jay," a la Julius Erving.

If he keeps jamming on opponents with regularity and ease, who knows? They might just be chanting it one day at JPJ.

# PART III
## Our Take

CRYSTAL GRAHAM

SCOTT RATCLIFFE

## ZACH PERELES
# Joy came in the morning

Kyle Guy had just settled into one of the cramped media breakout session areas deep inside U.S. Bank Stadium when he was asked a simple question.

*Why should the casual fan root for Virginia?*

After all, this was a Final Four of mainly new blood rather than blue blood. The Cavaliers were here for the first time since 1984. For Auburn, Virginia's opponent the next night, and Texas Tech, it was the first trip to this stage. And while Michigan State had been plenty of times, most recently in 2015, the Spartans hadn't won since 2000. Every team could claim the feel-good story angle for that reason and others.

Guy pondered the inquiry. He started his answer with how whether his team is liked or not isn't important. He then went into the unselfish playing style. And then he switched paths.

"We try to do it with a smile on our face," Guy said. "We've been through so much and have been doubted pretty much all of Coach [Tony] Bennett's tenure here."

To hear Guy say that was a major testament to his growth, because his lasting image for the previous 12 months had been him sobbing as UMBC celebrated in the background.

"I was hit with an overwhelming feeling of sadness, anxiety, and failure," Guy wrote in one of his famed letters to himself on Facebook. "While I was at half court and UMBC crowded the court I felt isolated. I was detached from reality. My brother, De'Andre Hunter, literally had to drag me and escort me off the court. As soon as I got in the locker room I hugged our seniors and I said 'I'm so sorry.' I went on to sit in the showers and cry alone."

But now there he was, beaming ear-to-ear the day before his matchup with Auburn. He couldn't stop smiling.

Not when he met with the media as an individual, not on the cart ride between to the main media room, not alongside Bennett and Ty Jerome once he got there, not as he fired up jumper after jumper, showed off some dance moves and energetically talked with his teammates at open practice, and not until he left U.S. Bank Stadium.

The next few days would include some harrowing experiences for the Cavaliers' championship quest. They trailed Auburn by four with under eight seconds left. They trailed Texas Tech by three with under 13 seconds left in regulation. And earlier, they had trailed Purdue with under a second remaining.

And yet, they came out of all of those games smiling. After beating the Tigers with three clutch free throws, Guy simply ran up the court with his arms raised until Austin Katstra lifted him up, an enduring image of the Cavaliers' resilience. After beating Texas Tech, Guy had a similar celebration, running and jumping for joy. This time, though, no one could catch him before he finally embraced Hunter and Jayden Nixon, the falling confetti surrounding him and his teammates on the hardwood.

"It means the world, and I wish I had the words, but it still does not feel real," Guy said after the game, as the clock ticked ever closer from Monday night to Tuesday morning.

A year earlier, Guy had published the words — so many words — that would help propel him forward following past failures. Now, at the peak of college basketball, he had none.

So, he laughed and smiled alongside Jerome, Hunter and Bennett. The entire group was beaming. And why wouldn't they have been? A year after suffering the most ignominious loss in sports history, they were champions — joyous champions. But joy for this Virginia team was there throughout the five-month season, not just after the championship was sealed.

Perhaps this group was especially joyous because "joy" was such a key word for them. Bennett quoted the Bible three years earlier, when the team lost to Syracuse, by saying, "Weeping may endure for the night, but joy comes in the morning." This entire season, when Bennett used "(t)he joy is in the competition" as a key point, has been that morning.

And so that's what I'll remember most from the campaign: the joy.

\*\*\*

It was five days later, and Guy was due for another press conference in another new room. This time, though, he faced a much smaller crowd on a much smaller stage. It was just him and Bennett together with several local and a few national reporters at Scott Stadium. It had been nearly a week since his team won, and he had claimed Final Four Most Outstanding Player honors. He had granted countless after-class picture requests and interview requests from around the nation. Still, it all felt so new, even back in the familiar old surroundings of his college home.

"I'm not sure if it's gonna settle in any time soon," Guy said. "For me, this is all so crazy. You dream of moments like this. It's been a little chaotic. … It's been fun. It comes with the territory, so I'm just trying to enjoy it all."

Guy and the rest of his teammates, along with the Virginia staff and managers, had just spent the previous few hours at the football stadium as part of their formal national championship celebration. Their basketball home, John Paul Jones Arena, was hosting another event, but even Bennett was dubious when told it wouldn't have been big enough to hold the expected crowd. All it took was one look, though, and the man who had made all the right decisions over the previous five months was proved wrong. The boisterous bunch of 21,000 wouldn't have had a chance to fit into JPJ.

"I'm blown away by it," Bennett said simply.

Then he took a more celebratory approach. As steady and calm as Bennett is in seemingly all scenarios, much less with a microphone in front of him, he knew today was a big moment for the community he had joined just over 10 years earlier.

"We played at Clemson, and we're riding up on the bus, and it was the time they were gonna celebrate the football national championship," Bennett said. "And we're riding up on the bus, and the stadium's full, and we're getting ready for our game, and I remember thinking, 'Man, what would that be like if we ever won a national championship?'"

He paused, if only for a moment, to gather himself for a very un-Tony-Bennett-like exclamation.

"And you know what? That day is now!"

The crowd erupted. Bennett marveled at it. This is what he had always intended to build when he arrived a decade ago and Virginia basketball attendance and interest was lacking. In his early years, he coached in front of half-empty John Paul Jones crowds. Now he was addressing a championship crowd too big for that venue.

He was now feeling the joy he had so long preached.

Of course, as quickly as those 21,000 fans had entered, and as quickly as they had erupted in cheers over and over again that afternoon, they just as rapidly exited the stadium, which, in turn, became completely quiet once again. If you hadn't been at Scott Stadium for those few hours, you might not have known there was even a celebration at all. But the day — and the months previous — will never be lost on those who experienced it.

"I'm kind of at a loss for words for what we've accomplished," Guy said.

Bennett shared in that feeling.

"I don't think, really, it has sunk in," Bennett said.

Perhaps it hadn't sunk in because when you work for something so hard for so long, it's a little strange when it's finally accomplished. The Cavaliers had no game plan to digest, no opposing offense to strangle, no opposing defense to dominate. They had accomplished all there is to accomplish. For the entire year prior, all this team had wanted was to win it all. What was left? For a program built on never resting on its laurels, it was a new situation. It was time, finally, to appreciate what had happened.

"I just think it'll get better and better," Bennett said.

\*\*\*

Sports, to me, are great because of the stories. Sure, box scores provide plenty of stories, and when those stories are great, the team is great. Virginia had a great team. It won a lot of games, posted lots of great scores and had plenty of players play well.

But as a storyteller, I'd like to think that sports has a more profound impact than the score. It is the players — the humanness — that brings meaning to the numbers you see on a scoreboard. That's why Virginia is a great team and a great champion but also why it is one of the best sports stories ever told.

So, I'll remember the moments that brought smiles and meaning.

I'll remember Kihei Clark dancing with the Battle 4 Atlantis mascot, a freshman growing into his comfort zone after the Cavaliers had clinched a trophy with a win over Wisconsin in late November. I'll remember Virginia returning from that tropical championship and defeating Maryland in College Park thanks to the man who, for five years, did the most thankless work: Jack Salt. I'll remember Bennett jumping out of his seat when Clark single-handedly forced a 10-second call against VCU. I'll remember team manager-turned-player Grant Kersey burying a turnaround three at the buzzer to give Virginia 100 points against Marshall, a victory that represented Bennett's 300th at the college level.

I'll remember Katstra draining a free throw at the end of a mid-January practice and being told that he had earned a scholarship, resulting in his teammates erupting.

The most meaningful moments don't always center on the most important players.

I'll remember Virginia blowing out Virginia Tech days later, a beatdown so thorough even some of the players, normally so humble, were quietly impressed with how well they had played. How could they not be? Virginia stayed undefeated longer than any other team in the nation.

But I'll also remember how they bounced back from losses. No team is perfect, and given how the previous season ended, Virginia had to be resilient. More importantly, they had to learn how to be resilient.

I'll remember Virginia, after suffering its first loss, at Duke, jumping out to a 25-3 lead against Wake Forest, burying the Demon Deacons from the start. I'll remember Virginia, after suffering another loss to Duke, bouncing back with an outstanding win at North Carolina, a game several Cavaliers pointed to as a key point in the season, two days later. I'll remember Virginia, after suffering a loss to Florida State in the ACC Tournament, realizing that while it was disappointing, it wasn't the end of the road. The team still had its biggest goal ahead. That type of poise could only come from the disappointments of Marches past.

After each loss, Virginia won at least six consecutive games. The six straight victories after the Florida State loss earned the Cavaliers a national championship.

More importantly, though, I'll remember the players. I'll remember Salt, who committed to Virginia before Bennett even had a single NCAA Tournament victory with the Cavaliers, staying level as ever in the minutes after the championship.

"I love basketball, but I know there's bigger things than basketball," Salt told me in a quiet corner of an exuberant post-game locker room. "This is great, but the connections I've made at this school, the bonds I've made with the players, coaches, staff, that's the biggest thing."

I'll remember Hunter and the little smile he'd carry with him down the court after scoring a basket. The bigger that smile grew, the bigger the trouble for the opponent. I'll remember Guy for the obvious reasons and Jerome for the obvious reasons, too. They were for the faces of the program when it lost to UMBC. They were, rightfully, the faces when it became national champions for the first time.

I'll remember Clark and how his 5-foot-9 frame stood tall in some of the most crucial moments. I'll remember Mamadi Diakite dyeing his hair blonde and blossoming into the shot-blocking and shot-making interior presence Bennett always knew he could become. I'll remember Jay Huff blocking helpless opponents' shots into oblivion and then smashing rims with thunderous dunks on the other end. I'll remember Braxton Key's ability to play any role needed of him, a trait most apparent when he played 29 huge minutes in the national championship.

Of course, this story is great, too, because of the time it took to come together. The construction of this roster goes back as far as six years before the championship, when Bennett first showed interest in Salt. But it also goes back to just days before the season started, when Key found out he'd be eligible. Along the way, Jerome, Guy and Clark filled in the backcourt, Hunter the wing and Diakite and Huff the interior. There was plenty of joy and plenty of sorrow.

For as long as it took to build this special group together, the members went different ways just as quickly. Hunter and Jerome declared their NBA intentions just weeks after the championship, and Guy and Diakite followed suit, while expressing they could still return for their senior seasons. (Guy later confirmed that he would remain in the draft, ending his time at UVA.) After 127 games, Salt will never don a Virginia uniform again. A lot of things change — that's the nature of college sports, after all — but not everything.

"Some things won't change," Bennett said. "We'll always be bonded together for life, but this will be special. I'm sure sometimes we'll be waddling out there 30 years from now when they commemorate the 2019 national championship team and all that.

"You watch [past] national championships … You know what? Virginia's now part of one of those memories."

Maybe, if I'm lucky, I'll waddle back to Charlottesville in 30 years, too, to remember this team and the joy it brought. I can't imagine a better way to be remembered.

# SCOTT RATCLIFFE
## Front row for the magical season

Long before I was covering the University of Virginia men's basketball program, I will admit it, I was a huge Cavalier hoops fan. Growing up the son of one of UVA's main beat writers for decades, some of my best moments in life have fallen in direct connection with Wahoo athletics.

My first real sports memory was Ralph Sampson's last game at University Hall in 1983, when he got his own rebound off a missed free throw and scored on a putback to beat Maryland.

I was hooked.

My life from then on revolved around Terry Holland and the hoops program, George Welsh and the football team, and pretty much all things UVA athletics. Being Jerry Ratcliffe's son, I often knew "the scoop" on a second-hand basis.

Among my heroes growing up were guys like Richard Morgan, Bryant Stith, John Crotty, Cory Alexander, Curtis Staples, Junior Burrough and many others. Into my college years, I still followed the program very closely and went to as many games as I could even when I no longer resided in Central Virginia.

I was there for the double-overtime comeback win at Cameron Indoor Stadium in 1995. The "Last Ball in U-Hall" and the first game at JPJ. There when Pete Gillen, Roger Mason, Travis Watson and the 'Hoos lost to Gonzaga in Memphis in 2001. There when Sean Singletary and J.R. Reynolds fell short against Tennessee in Columbus in 2007. I witnessed first-hand several Cavalier first-round, heartbreaking exits in the ACC Tournament over the years as well.

My mom, Dianne, and I attended countless UVA games together over the years. She's the biggest Wahoo I know, and was right by my side through all the ups and downs of being a Virginia supporter.

My friend Anthony Esposito, another longtime Virginia fan that I've known since kindergarten, was with me at the VCU game at John Paul Jones Arena in 2013 when the Rams stole one at the end, and I asked, "When will this ever end?"

I hung out with Anthony and his brother, Matt, another huge Wahoo fan, just before this year's national championship game at Pog Mahone's in Minneapolis (along with my good Cavalier friends, Amy and Jason Porter) and we agreed that, "It ends now."

Behind Malcolm Brogdon, Joe Harris and Justin Anderson, the Cavaliers officially put themselves back on the college basketball map in 2014, in one of the top moments in Wahoo history. UVA defeated Jabari Parker and Duke to win their first ACC Tournament in 38 years.

Anthony, Jason and I celebrated that one in style afterwards while watching the announcement on Selection Sunday. Hours later, ahead of a nasty snowstorm in Greensboro, the 'Hoos were selected as a No. 1 seed.

The next step was getting back to the Final Four. We all remember the heartache after the Wahoos lost two years in a row at the hands of Tom Izzo and Michigan State, then the blown lead against Syracuse in Chicago in 2016 that temporarily erased that little glimmer of hope that the 'Hoos were finally going to take that next step.

The following season ended with one of the most forgettable, lopsided losses Cavalier fans can recall, when Florida dismantled UVA in the second round. Then, the ultimate disappointment last season in Charlotte against that four-letter school from the state to the north that we won't mention right now.

Which all led up to this unforgettable ride of a season, my first on the UVA hoops "beat."

I had covered Virginia basketball games here and there over the years for other media outlets as a stringer or correspondent, when those said outlets didn't send a writer but wanted a first-hand account of the team they covered against the 'Hoos.

I quickly adjusted to the concept of shedding my love for the Cavaliers at the stadium/arena entrance and covering each game with an unbiased view. It was awkward at times during games when in years past I'd be yelling, "Come on, defense!" or "That's a horrible call, ref!" and now I had to just sit in silence and take notes.

Any kind of cheering from the press box is widely known as a no-no that could cost you your media pass, so I'd sit there, at times going crazy inside my head, and put together a game story, usually for Virginia's opponent's newspaper. It was quite an adjustment, but I realized it was something I'd have to do if I wanted to be in the sportswriting business.

Fast forward to this summer. My father had just jump-started his new business, JerryRatcliffe.com, and I gladly hopped aboard. The idea of covering Virginia sports and having Dad as my boss was too great to pass up.

I've never considered myself anything close to a great writer, and still don't. But I figured I'd be learning from the best, from a guy who's been through this rodeo over 40 years and could show me the ropes.

We went through the first half of UVA football season together when, in early October, it really hit me — in like a month, I'm going to be covering a top-10 basketball team for an entire season, and that team just happens to be the same team I've followed closer and have cared most about, more than any other team in any other sport, for the majority of my existence. It didn't feel real. Still doesn't, really.

Fast forward to late October in Charlotte, N.C., a city I lived in for two years and loved. As it turns out, it would be the place where my coverage of UVA basketball officially began with ACC Operation Basketball, where players and coaches from all 15 schools come together to discuss the upcoming season.

Heading into the Spectrum Center, I felt like I had finally arrived as a member of the sports media. Even after going through a similar event (in Charlotte, no less) a few months earlier for the ACC football preseason, basketball — particularly UVA and ACC basketball — has always been my true love and passion, for as long as I can remember.

It was bittersweet to hear Tony Bennett, Kyle Guy and Jack Salt rehash the infamous defeat on the same floor that abruptly ended their stellar 2017-2018 season. But just as they had done immediately after the fact, the Wahoo representatives handled each question with grace, dignity, and respectability. You could start to get a sense that these guys were going to use the frustration and turn it into motivation, and propel themselves to a new plateau.

You just had a feeling — even in October — that this team really had a chance to do something special, and boy, did this group do just that. In years past, there was always that one Kentucky team or that Michigan State or Duke or Villanova team that seemed to be on another level.

At the start of the 2018-2019 campaign, all the talk was about the Blue Devils and their trio of talented one-and-done freshmen. But deep down, this was the first year I could ever remember when there wasn't a single team in the country that I felt Virginia should be worried about. As it panned out, Duke swept the 'Hoos in a pair of tightly contested primetime battles, and what Wahoo Nation wouldn't have given for one more shot at Coach K's troops in the postseason. But still, I felt all along that when these Cavaliers really buckled down and played their best basketball, they could beat anybody, anywhere, any time.

They proved that with a pair of three-point barrages against Florida State and Virginia Tech, two teams both ranked in the top 10 nationally, early in the ACC slate, then later showed their fight and resilience on the road in near-impossible situations at N.C. State, North Carolina, Louisville and Syracuse.

The ACC Tournament loss to FSU was disappointing for most Cavalier fans, but ultimately didn't affect the team's No. 1 seeding in the Big Dance.

The ultimate goal was still in clear view. Six wins, and you're a champion.

Sitting at Colonial Life Arena in Columbia, S.C., during the first-round matchup against 16th-seeded Gardner-Webb, there was a moment of doubt that the 'Hoos would be able rally from that 14-point deficit or face further humiliation with another embarrassing loss.

And that's about the time that the true Cavaliers showed up. It was as if "Uncle Mo" had gotten stuck in traffic, but showed up just in time to put a much-needed charge into the 'Hoos.

After displaying the true meaning of "Survive and Advance," Bennett's boys held off a hot bunch from Oklahoma to advance to Louisville and the Sweet Sixteen.

Arriving at the KFC Yum! Center a week later, it started to feel more realistic that UVA could make it through to Minneapolis. Oregon, a Cinderella-story 12-seed, put up its best fight, but the 'Hoos prevailed and advanced onto the South Region championship against No. 3 Purdue.

Three down, three to go. Halfway there. But wow, that Purdue team looked extremely impressive in its overtime win over a tough, second-seeded Tennessee squad. The Boilermaker backcourt duo of Carsen Edwards and Ryan Cline went off from three-point land against the Vols, and everyone knew it was going to be a tall task to outlast them in the regional final.

I was blessed to be seated on the front row in the corner on the baseline across from Virginia's bench for both games in Louisville. One of the best seats in the house. Had to pinch myself a couple times. I was going to be sitting courtside for arguably the biggest UVA game in over 30 years. And what a game it was.

The 'Hoos and Boilermakers went blow for blow in a heavyweight bout. Edwards was sensational. Half of West Lafayette was there dressed in black and gold, and they got really loud at times. Things didn't look so good for the Cavaliers when Cline headed to the free-throw line with a chance to make it a two-possession game and put Purdue up by four points with 17 ticks showing in regulation.

I glanced over at the UVA bench and loyal fans sitting behind them, and there were signs of that all-too-familiar, dejected look — not again.

Then, it happened.

The play. One of the most, if not the most, amazing plays in college basketball memory. Ty Jerome stepped to the line for two shots with just 5.9 seconds remaining, with Virginia trailing by three, and the dream hanging by a thread. After hitting the first, Jerome's second free throw bounced off the rim, and Mamadi Diakite tapped the ball into the backcourt.

Without hesitation, freshman point guard Kihei Clark quickly chased the ball down, grabbed it, looked off Jerome and Guy, two of the country's deadliest shooters, and instead looked ahead to Diakite, about 12 feet from the hoop, with time dwindling down.

Diakite may not have been known for his outside shot, but he had the best look at the potential game-tying basket.

Clark lasered his long delivery pass to Diakite, who in one motion caught and quickly released the ball in the nick of time to beat the clock and swish it through, saving the season and sending the game into overtime.

And it happened right in front of me.

Moments later, it was those wearing orange and blue that were celebrating their team's first trip to the Final Four in decades, 35 years to be exact. I was not worthy to have a front-row seat for that.

I was six years old the last time UVA had advanced to the Final Four, so I barely remember the game, the scenes from it, the memories. It was surreal to come to the realization that not only would the 'Hoos be heading to the Final Four, but that I'd be going with them. An item on the ol' bucket list was checked off, but I never knew for sure if it would be Virginia that was one of the participants if I ever really did make it to a Final Four.

For me, one of the most memorable parts of the trip to Minneapolis was the trip itself. Long story short, I was in a car accident when I was 18 years old that left me paralyzed from the chest down. For this reason, I hadn't flown much since, only a couple of times, and a pretty long time ago.

So, Dad and I decided we would drive to Minnesota, a 17½-hour voyage nearly halfway across the country. We hopped on 64 West and ventured through West Virginia and Kentucky, then up through Ohio, Indiana, Illinois and Wisconsin, where we stopped Wednesday night, about an hour and a half away from our destination.

We arrived in the Twin Cities Thursday afternoon for team press conferences and interviews at the cavernous U.S. Bank Stadium, and it really hit me then and there.

You're at the freakin' Final Four, man!

All those times seeing the Final Four press conferences and thinking how cool it would be to see a Virginia logo slapped up there behind the podium had become a reality. Bennett and the players talked about going up against Auburn in the semifinals, getting adjusted to the sight lines of the court — which was essentially placed on top of an NFL football field, and were still having to answer questions about last season.

There were more interviews Friday, and then the day finally came. Virginia was back in the Final Four, and it was the early game for a change after so many late-night finishes.

Auburn was the hottest team in the country, having just defeated Kansas, North Carolina and Kentucky all in a row to punch their ticket, even after losing a key piece in Chuma Okeke to injury against the Tar Heels. The Tigers, who had won 12 straight games and 14 of their last 15 heading into the Final Four, were still a force to be reckoned with, no doubt. Bryce Brown and Jared Harper were one of the top backcourt duos in the country.

It looked like easy sailing when the 'Hoos went up 10 with 5:21 to go, but the Tigers showed why they'd gotten that far, reeling off 14 points in a row to take a four-point lead with only 17.6 seconds to play.

Once again, I glanced over at the Virginia fans sitting behind the baseline and saw that same old look from a few, as if to say, "You've got to be kidding me."

But Guy was not to be denied, scoring six points in the final 7.4 seconds.

Again, I was blessed to sit in the corner, front row on the baseline. In the same corner where Guy was fouled by Samir Doughty with just six-tenths of a second left, the same corner where the celebration spilled over at game's end after he nailed all three pressure-packed free throws.

And just like that, once again, when it looked impossible, when the odds were completely stacked against them, the Cavaliers pulled through — only this time, they were heading to the national championship. Didn't feel real, still doesn't.

That unforgettable Monday evening in Minneapolis provided more of the same heart-pounding excitement, seeing the 'Hoos grab the early lead, only to have the Red Raiders make a late surge and pull ahead in the closing minutes of regulation.

That is, until Ty Jerome drove and dished out to De'Andre Hunter for his triple that sent the game to overtime, where Virginia dominated the final five minutes and celebrated the first national title in program history.

The orange-and-blue clad party had begun on the court. Bennett slapped "Virginia" onto the champion spot on the bracket on the podium, "One Shining Moment" rang through the building. One by one, the 'Hoos cut down the nets with alumni there to congratulate them.

All of these memories that will be forever etched in Wahoo history were happening right in front of me, and it was indescribable. It was literally like living a dream, from the moment I first entered U.S. Bank Stadium until the last stroll through the skywalk back to the media parking garage early Tuesday morning. None of it felt real, still doesn't.

Sitting in the UVA championship locker room after the win waiting on Guy, the Most Outstanding Player, I thought about what I was going to ask him.

I figured I'd only get one question in, as he was mobbed from every direction, three or four reporters deep, microphones and tape recorders everywhere. I had microphone wires, pens and notebooks in my face, people shoving me.

My window had arrived, as there was enough of a break in the questioning for me to ask Guy what he'd like to say to all the doubters, all the naysayers, all the haters who said this team wasn't capable of such a run, and he summed it up in two words.

"Thank you," he said.

Yes, Virginia won it all. Fans who were watching at JPJ rushed the floor, with the team they loved celebrating on a different floor hundreds of miles away. The Corner went wild into the wee hours of Tuesday morning. The whole country will remember the Cavaliers' ride for years to come.

But the story behind it all — of how the team fought through unprecedented adversity and it used it time and time again to fuel the most memorable run in the proud history of UVA basketball — you couldn't have scripted it any better.

# SCOTT GERMAN
# Happy for an old friend

I wasn't supposed to be in Charlottesville that day. Actually, I was supposed to be in Minneapolis, getting ready to watch my beloved Virginia Cavaliers men's basketball team play in their first ever national championship game.

Did I mention that it was their FIRST-EVER NATIONAL CHAMPIONSHIP GAME?

You see, it was only fitting for me to be in Minneapolis. I've been following this program for a long time. I have followed Virginia basketball since my dad carried me into University Hall just a few games after the inaugural game against the University of Kentucky in 1964.

(The fact that my dad carried me in his arms into U-Hall is a story within itself, which I feel compelled to expand on later).

I followed this team throughout the glory years of Virginia basketball, with Ralph Sampson dominating the hardwood. I am proud to say that I never missed a home game during the four years that Ralph wore No. 50. I followed this program before Barry Parkhill drilled his historic baseline jumper to beat sixth-ranked South Carolina in 1971. I attended two Final Fours, 1981 and 1984, respectively. And I did all this "following" both as a fan and sportswriter.

I was destined, no, I was determined to be in Minneapolis on Monday night, April 8, 2019.

Nothing, I mean NOTHING, would stop me.

Nothing except acute bronchitis and a caring wife who insisted that I stay home and rest.

Are you kidding me? Stay home? Rest? Miss the national championship, THE NATIONAL CHAMPIONSHIP, that my revered Cavaliers were appearing in, and that I have literally waited for my entire life?

Can't make it up. I waved the white flag of surrender. I was too sick to travel. I remained in Virginia and watched as my friends and colleagues began to depart for THE game.

I was heartbroken, to say the least.

Sometimes, life hands us opportunities, and those opportunities end up being gifts. We may not fully comprehend why things happen the way they do, but in the end, I was exactly where I was supposed to be.

I decided that despite not being courtside with close friends and thousands of fellow Cavalier faithful, I was determined to make the best of the situation as it was presented to me. And at the end of the night, and well into Tuesday morning, I found an inner peace.

In Charlottesville, in John Paul Jones Arena, just mere steps away from where all of my UVA basketball memories began as a child. This time, however, I was with my own son. My adult son, Andrew, who has also become a follower of my team.

(Of course, he is a Wahoo.)

Monday morning, April 8, 2019, for me was just a continuation of Sunday, April 7, 2019, which was a mere continuation of Saturday, April 6, 2019, the evening of the heart-stopping win over Auburn in the NCAA semifinals.

You remember the game, the one where time froze in the life of every Virginia Cavalier basketball fan, frozen solid during all three of Kyle Guy's swished free throws, and as Auburn's last-second desperation shot fell harmlessly short, sending Virginia to its first-ever national championship game.

I watched the game along with Andrew from the UVA Amphitheater with a couple thousand diehard Cavalier fans, students and townspeople alike. We watched in disbelief and horror as Virginia saw a 10-point lead late in the game evaporate, Auburn going on a 14-0 run to take what appeared to be an insurmountable four-point advantage inside of 10 seconds left.

An insurmountable lead to almost any team in the nation not named Virginia.

You know how it turned out, storybook ending, heart-stopping, and a victory for the Cardiac Cavaliers.

Ho hum, been there, done that.

Now onto Monday night, the 8th of April, 2019. It was time to prepare for another date with destiny, a date with the Texas Tech Red Raiders.

In the interest of full disclosure, I feel I should tell you that I am a little superstitious, and have a very obsessive-compulsive personality. These two traits can potentially be a lethal combination, especially if you are both a college basketball fan and a fan of the Virginia Cavaliers men's basketball team.

I leave nothing for chance. I make sure I stick to a similar game-day routine, I wear the appropriate clothing, and I plan my departure time, allowing for an unplanned event that could cause me to be late.

Above all else, I have my mind in the right place, a place that can handle either a win or a loss.

Who am I kidding? I am never prepared for a loss, especially a loss in the national championship game.

Not possible, ever!

So, on this Monday morning, I decided I was going to prepare for the game as methodically as I knew Coach Tony Bennett and his staff had done.

I was thrilled to learn that John Paul Jones Arena was showing the game for students and the community.

Bronchitis aside, there was no doubt that this was where both my son and I would be.

JPJ opened at 8 p.m. for the 9:20 p.m. tip-off. I decided I would get there early to ensure that I didn't miss a thing.

First thing I did was confirm with my son, who resides in Waynesboro, that he was indeed going to man-up and meet me in Charlottesville to endure with me what was sure to be another 40 minutes of pure torture on both our parts.

We had somehow survived the epic battle in the Amphitheater on Saturday night, and to do it all over again felt normal to me, but I wanted to make sure he was on board.

I explained to Andrew that he needed to be in Charlottesville by at least 5 p.m. Seems logical, right? Doesn't everyone show up three hours before the doors even open to watch a game on a giant television screen?

Keep in mind that the actual team is playing the game some 1,100 miles away.

Yep, that's what my way of thinking is all about, and evidently the apple does not fall far from the tree, as his reply was, "Why so late?"

By now it's Monday, mid-morn. We knew where we were watching the game, and we had cemented a meeting time.

Oh crud, where will I park? I warned you that I was determined to make this day as nerve-wracking as I possibly could. There was no chance whatsoever that I was going to make the drive from my Fluvanna County residence and simply stroll into Charlottesville three hours early without a plan.

That's not my style.

At this point, I decided the only logical way to prepare for this was to do a dry run. So, I got in my car and drove the 20-plus-mile drive into Charlottesville to do some pre-game scouting.

I first drove to the arena and promptly found a University of Virginia police officer and asked about available parking for the viewing of the contest. The officer advised me that the JPJ lots would all be open and free to park.

Great! I will be at JPJ early enough for the ultimate parking spot.

Thanking the officer, I started to return to my car, and as I was walking, I glanced over at the chain-linked fence that barricades University Hall.

I returned to the police officer and asked if I could park in the U-Hall lot. His reply: "Sure thing."

It could not be more perfect. I would park where my earliest memories of

SCOTT GERMAN

Virginia basketball started for me as a toddler in 1964.

OK, so, "toddler" is a bit of a stretch. Considering I was born in March 1957, by the time December '64 rolled around, I was about seven and half years old.

Remember, earlier, I wrote about my dad, Bill, who introduced me to this madness called Cavalier basketball? Remember I told you how he carried me through the turnstiles of University Hall?

Funny thing, I have spent most my adult life wondering why, at the age of seven and a half, and fairly large for my age, I might add, my dad would have picked me up like a sack of potatoes and carried me into the arena?

The answer to my question came unexpectedly a few years ago when I was discussing the early days of U-Hall with a true Cavalier legend, James "Monk" Bingler.

Monk had been associated with UVA in various capacities for over 80 years. Sadly, Monk passed away in 2018.

When I asked Monk why he thought my dad had carried me into U Hall at an age where I could obviously walk in on my own (remember, I was seven and a half!), he instantly knew the reason.

Monk told me that during that time, young children who were carried in by their parents were admitted to the games for free. Seems that policy was loosely enforced by UVA, as the staff wanted all the warm bodies they could possibly fit into University Hall.

Monk's family and my dad's family lived in close proximity to one another in Charlottesville. The families were not well-off; saving money was key. Monk helped me to see that my dad wanted to share his love of UVA basketball with his son, while saving a penny or two.

Back to the checklist, then.

Watch location, check.

Watch partner, check.

Meeting time, check.

Parking spot, check.

It would appear that my pre-game scouting was complete, right? Wrong! Believing that the Cavs would pull off a win at some time around midnight on Monday, I needed to map out a direct route that would get me to the intersection of University Avenue and 14th Street, The Corner.

I knew thousands would be at The Corner celebrating after the game. I was not going to miss the celebration, but I felt sure that many streets around The Corner would be closed.

I needed to have a plan that would ensure that I could get to the aforementioned location from JPJ in an expeditious manner. I was not going to walk, run, or even ride one of those green scooters I have seen around town.

I am in my 60s, and I have my dignity. I was going to drive and park within close proximity of the celebration.

I was on a mission.

For the next two hours, I drove around Charlottesville like a Google Earth vehicle lurking in back alleys, people's yards, and yes, even a rooftop.

Just as I had hoped, I found a perfect driving route, and a safe and legal parking spot, that was just steps away from The Corner.

On a side note, I anticipate celebrating again next year in the same fashion, so I won't be sharing my route or spot with anyone.

Now, on to the game itself. You know how the story goes, it was the same all tournament long. UVA starts off sluggish, heats up, pulls away, goes up in flames, and then pulls off a miraculous rally to win in the waning tenths of seconds.

And, true to form, the Cavaliers did win on Monday night. Despite needing an overtime, they actually secured the win long before the clock struck 0:00. They became the national champions with an 85-77 win over Texas Tech.

What is ironic about this game? All season long I sat beside my colleague and friend, Chris Graham, editor of AugustaFreePress.com, on press row in John Paul Jones Arena, and other venues.

Chris, bless his heart, spent an entire season attempting to reason with me, coaxing me, talking me off the ledge, especially when things were going sideways for the Wahoos.

Just because I am a sportswriter doesn't mean I could be rational. I was as panic-stricken as any other fan. Truth is, I also I felt I had earned a right to display these behaviors, as I was in the Charlotte Spectrum last March when that very bad thing happened.

That was the night that I, along with my friends, packed up our toys and drove home immediately after our team lost to UMBC.

It was a long, grueling five-hour drive home that lasted early into the next morning.

But during the game on April 8, 2019, it was my turn to be the calm mentor to my son.

I found myself repeating over and over to him, "We have this," even though in my mind I felt as though the world was coming to an end.

Seriously.

To my surprise, I must have done OK. Andrew and I survived to the end, we celebrated together. We celebrated along with approximately 14,000 Cavalier fans watching inside JPJ. And we celebrated outside the arena, where there was joy everywhere you looked.

We created memories. Memories that will last us for a lifetime.

We created memories just like my dad and I had done decades before.

\*\*\*

After the celebration, Andrew and I said our goodbyes. As I made the walk back across the street to University Hall towards my car, I was faced with reality.

Not just the reality of my team winning the national championship, but also the reality of having to say farewell to a dear old friend, University Hall. A place that, in my memory, was once the center of the college basketball universe, but now sits alone in darkness and silence.

I reflected how this grand building has survived through the years. I am glad that University Hall was still standing on a day that will live forever in UVA and Charlottesville history.

And so, on the final night, of the Final Four, I had my last shining moment with University Hall, standing feet away from the main entrance.

With tears in my eyes, I said my final goodbye.

"You have served us well, dear friend," I said, out loud, not caring if anyone heard, and thought it strange that a grown man appeared to be muttering to himself.

"What a journey it has been."

## CHRIS GRAHAM
# Emotions flow as Virginia makes history

I am not ashamed to admit that the tears were flowing for me as the final seconds counted down in Minneapolis as UVA Basketball wrapped its first national title.

OK, sure, basketball, football – sports, in general – mere diversions, get that.

Somebody has to win the championship.

They give one out every year, in every sport.

Your favorite team winning one doesn't make them or you any more special than the team that won last year, the one that wins next year, the rest.

But it does make you feel special, and it's been a long time since I figured out why, and why I let myself get emotional over these things.

Following a sports team is a way to let yourself be a part of something bigger.

For some, that something bigger is religion; for others, politics, though, gotta say, you politics people, and I used to be one of you, so I can speak from experience, y'all are freaks.

Sports isn't life or death.

(Neither are religion or politics. At least sports knows it isn't life or death.)

I spent the next day in Minnesota because, unlike practically everybody else in the media contingent that covers UVA Athletics, I couldn't get a flight out, because I couldn't get there until the day of the national semifinals due to my obligations broadcasting ESPN college baseball.

Which, fine. My wife, Crystal, got her hands on national championship T-shirts and hats at U.S. Bank Stadium, so we threw those on and spent the day at the Mall of America, just walking around.

I've never been, may never be back, and Crystal is a native Minnesotan, and after spending the day between the semifinals and the championship game in her hometown, Owatonna, a city of around 25,000 residents about an hour south of Minneapolis, farm country, she wanted to show me the touristy side.

We could barely walk 10 feet without running into other UVA fans leaving town either that night or the next day and sharing.

And that was around me taking phone calls from my college roommate, Jay Whitaker, who might be a bigger UVA sports fan than me, which is saying a lot; and Scott German, who couldn't be here with us because he came down with bronchitis earlier in the postseason, and might be a bigger UVA sports fan than Jay.

I did a radio interview with Mark Moses, who hosts a daily sports talk show in Central Florida, and who I'd met years ago when we sat beside each other in the press box at Scott Stadium, when he was producing for a local radio station, dreaming of hosting his own show one day.

I traded texts with Wade Branner, the Voice of VMI Athletics, who covered for me so that I could shove out of town, doing a pair of weekend ESPN broadcasts of VMI baseball solo.

Friends from back home who I know aren't otherwise sports fans sent messages of congratulations, and wrote about how they'd watched the game, and what an exciting game it was, and how cool it was that UVA had pulled the game out.

That's what gets me, in terms of the emotions.

It's thinking about all the people involved, whatever level of involved they were, and knowing what it meant to for so many of them to see their favorite team finally win the big game.

Or, would have meant to them.

My mother, for instance, God rest her soul.

She used to tell me the story of when I first used to tell people that I was going to go to school at UVA.

My sister, four years younger, had some issues at birth, and we spent a lot of time back and forth between Charlottesville and the Valley as the folks at UVA Hospital did their magic.

So, I wasn't even in elementary school yet, telling people, I'm going to go to school at UVA, though, oddly, according to Mom, I didn't aim to be a doctor, but rather, a lawyer.

I had a plan. I was going to be governor of Virginia, then, president.

I'd schemed this up at age 4.

I was an odd kid.

CRYSTAL GRAHAM

Then, in second grade, a guy named Ralph Sampson began his matriculation on Grounds.

Now, the plan was amended. I was going to play basketball for Terry Holland, then governor, then the presidency.

Big dreams for a kid growing up in a rural trailer park, but I didn't know then that kids growing up in a rural trailer park weren't supposed to dream big.

(Lucky for me, I didn't know any of that until I'd already graduated from UVA.)

Back to elementary school: I had a strict bedtime: 9 p.m.

Except that Mom knew how much I loved UVA Basketball, so, when the 'Hoos were on TV on a weeknight, I could stay up past 9, as long as I promised to get up in the morning and go to school, no matter how late the game went.

(One triple-overtime game ended at midnight. Virginia won; school was rough the next day.)

Mom did allow me to be, ahem, sick, on the Friday of the ACC Tournament, except for seventh grade.

The school screwed up that year, and scheduled the spelling bee for the Friday of the ACC Tournament.

I was the two-time defending champion. Couldn't be sick that day.

Good news: I won, and so did UVA.

A teacher, knowing my allegiances, made sure that I was in on that news as soon as the spelling bee was over.

I thought of my mom when I was on the floor at U.S. Bank Stadium.

She would have stayed up and watched, and then called or texted to ask me what it was like to be on the court for the celebration and then in the locker room to do interviews.

She always used to call me when I was at ACC Tournaments.

And told everybody she knew about how her son had written a book on the history of UVA basketball.

She was so proud.

She passed away in 2015.

I regret that she didn't live to hear how happy I was when Virginia finally won the national title.

I also thought of Scott German's father, Bill, who passed away in 2016.

Bill worked for many years as an usher at UVA Athletics events, and started taking his sons to games and got them hooked.

He had a major health scare at the end of the 2013-2014 season, and then accompanied Scott and I to an early-season game that November.

Hanging around after the game to wait for us to do our job interviewing players, he struck up a conversation with two gentlemen who happened to be relatives of UVA star Justin Anderson, and who motioned for Justin to come up from courtside after doing a postgame radio interview to say hello to the nice man who was a long-time fan.

Long story short, Justin Anderson had been the big player that night, and us reporter types were back in the locker room waiting for him to come back so we could ask important questions about basketball, but he ended up in conversation with Bill for going on 20 minutes, because that was more important at the time.

And, no doubt, it was.

I thought of Bill as "One Shining Moment" started up in the arena, and Justin Anderson.

And Malcolm Brogdon, and Joe Harris, who were, like Anderson, in U.S. Bank Stadium for the title game, and without whom none of what happened would have been possible.

Malcolm, Joe, Justin – London Perrantes, Isaiah Wilkins, Devon Hall, Anthony Gill, Mike Tobey, Darion Atkins, Akil Mitchell – they weren't recruited to win 30 games and ACC championships and No. 1 NCAA Tournament seeds.

They were the kind of recruits that a program that wins 20 games and watches Joe Lunardi bracketology updates to see if they're going to get a bid ends up landing.

Who worked their butts off to take it to the next level, which in turn made it possible for Tony Bennett and his staff to be able to tap into higher-level recruits.

I'll always say that the loss that stings me most as a fan is not the UMBC defeat from 2018 that we all talk about so much, but instead the 2016 Elite

Eight loss to Syracuse, because the key guys on that team were seniors, they should have been the one to break through, they are all such great people, and it ended too soon.

I think about those folks.

I think about a lot of folks that I don't know, but whose stories are similar to mine, what it means to them.

We all, as fans, get together with our people 15-20 times a year for home games, some road games, tournament games, we keep up with each other for the other games that we don't watch together, we talk about it when we talk, and the end goal is to see your team win the big game.

And then, finally, it happens.

As it's happening, on a magical Monday night in April, I'm thinking about the people that I've shared this silly obsession with, the ones who aren't here with us anymore to be able to enjoy it with us, the ones who made it possible, the ones who made them possible.

And then, I tear up.

I'm not too cool for school to admit that.

# JERRY RATCLIFFE
# Happiness for others as Virginia wins title

I've been blessed throughout my career in sports journalism to have witnessed so many dramatic, improbable, thrilling moments, many of them history-making feats in both team and individual events.

Super Bowls, U.S. Opens, Major League Baseball, the Masters, NASCAR, professional boxing, college bowl games and national championships, college baseball, tennis, lacrosse, track & field, soccer, and college basketball, particularly Final Fours, have all been checked off my list, some of them many times over.

You learn from the beginning in professional sports journalism that the first rules of thumb are "no cheering in the press box," and to remain unbiased in your writing/reporting. In a short time, one builds an immunity to emotion. That's how they describe a grizzled veteran.

As a sportswriter, what you're rooting for is a good story, one that you hope is so delicious that it would be difficult to screw it up.

While writers may have bias, it isn't supposed to show. You may personally dislike a coach, a player, a team. You may admire a coach, a player, a team. The reader isn't supposed to be able to tell the difference.

We are there to tell the story, often one that the TV cameras can't capture, behind the scenes stuff. Why things happened. What participants thought about this or that. Paint a picture for the reader, give them something they can't get anywhere else.

My story of the 2019 Final Four may be a little different than my colleagues that offered up their feelings in this book. I didn't get emotional, didn't shed any tears, didn't celebrate. Instead, I tried to tell the story the best I could and put a perspective on it after having covered many Final Fours in my career, and 37 years of covering Virginia athletics.

The emotion I could offer was happiness for others.

I was happy for the 15,000-plus in my company's (JerryRatcliffe.com) social media family and supporters of my website and radio show. I was happy for so many close friends. I was happy for my family, almost all of whom reside in Charlottesville, most of them having grown up here. My oldest daughter got a special birthday present in that the national championship arrived on her birthday.

I was happy for my son, Jon Scott, who because I dragged my family to Charlottesville in 1982, they all grew up in a sports household and naturally became Virginia fans. Scott, who felt the lure of sportswriting just like his old man, and I made the epic trips throughout the postseason together, including to Minneapolis, an unforgettable journey we can share for years to come.

I was happy for Tony Bennett, to finally prove his critics wrong. I was happy for his coaching staff, especially Jason Williford, who I covered in 1995 when he was part of a Jeff Jones-coached team that came oh-so-close to reaching the Final Four.

I was happy for all former players, particularly the ones that came as close as Williford. This championship belonged to all of those people that helped build Virginia's program to its present status.

Lastly, I was happy for Wahoo Nation.

I have covered Final Fours and national championships in college football and basketball and witnessed the euphoria experienced by followers of those programs. There's nothing quite like winning a Natty.

Having chronicled UVA sports from the press box or press row for nearly four decades, I've witnessed too much heartbreak, too much pain for one college program to bear. If you're a UVA fan – and you most surely are if you're reading this book – you can relate.

How many times have Wahoo fans been on the brink of exhilaration, jubilation, celebration, only to have their bubble burst? So many times and in so many ways, sometimes odds-defying ways, Virginia has snatched defeat from the jaws of victory.

If you need any kind of reminder, I recall the 1990 football loss to Georgia Tech when the No. 1 ranked and undefeated Cavaliers should have won that game and had numerous opportunities to do so. There was the 1983 loss to N.C. State in the NCAA West Region Finals when Ralph Sampson's Cavaliers were hands-down the best team in the nation.

As mentioned earlier, Jones' '95 team came close to touching the Final Four, having knocked off favorite Kansas in its own backyard, only to run out of gas against Nolan Richardson's "Forty Minutes of Hell" Razorbacks team.

Who will ever forget the collapse against Syracuse in the Elite Eight a few years back in Chicago? Talk about a lock.

The Cavaliers were so far ahead of Jim Boeheim's Orange that I was filling out Final Four media credential requests and booking hotels and flights online at halftime. My editor at the time, Nick Mathews, one of the best I've ever worked with, had already put together a great game plan for coverage at the Final Four in Houston.

By the end of the second half, I was frantically canceling all those reservations as Virginia fans watched in disbelief as the Cavaliers suffered a monumental collapse.

So, for all those who had their hearts broken over the years, I was delighted for them to have their "One Shining Moment" that no one can ever take away.

Finally, it was very cool to write a happy ending to a Virginia story. There have been many over the years, but none to this scale. This time it was for all the marbles and the Cavaliers collected.

The more this storyline moved along, with all the fabulous endings that only a Hollywood script writer could imagine, this team more and more began to remind me of Jim Valvano's magical ride in 1983, stealing a Final Four spot from Virginia and stunning a highly-favored, much more talented Houston Phi Slama Jama team in the national championship.

Jimmy V's Wolfpack kept pulling off one miracle after another until it left him running wildly on the court in Albuquerque, looking for someone to hug.

That's why I wrote in advance of Virginia's title, that I predicted the Cavaliers would win it all because it was a "Team of Destiny," just like Jimmy V's.

When Virginia defeated Texas Tech in overtime, I took advantage of my media privilege to walk onto the floor as the confetti floated from the ceiling, and started recording the historic moment with my nifty cell-phone camera, capturing the players and coaches cutting down the net.

SCOTT RATCLIFFE

JERRY RATCLIFFE

I had never witnessed that much joy in the afterglow of a Virginia win before. It was nice to see the smiles, tears of joy, replace the ones of sorrow from so many locker rooms past.

As the U.S. Bank Stadium sound system blared the traditional "One Shining Moment," and the players and everyone remaining in the arena stopped to watch, I video recorded Kyle Guy, De'Andre Hunter, and Ty Jerome, huddled together below their teammates, taking it all in.

I couldn't help but wonder what must have been going through their minds at that moment. Overcoming situations that seemed near impossible to get there, then to pull it off, to win it all … my God. It would definitely be the last time they would play together, most likely the last time at least two of them would wear the Virginia uniform.

Thank goodness I'm a grizzled veteran, or emotions might have gotten the best of me. Instead, I was destined to go and try to put down on paper what was a really good story, and just hoped I didn't screw it up.

237

# ABOUT THE AUTHORS

**Jerry Ratcliffe** is the dean of the UVA sports media, having covered the 'Hoos and ACC basketball for 45 years. The four-time Virginia Sportswriter of the Year, as selected by the National Sportscasters and Sportswriters Association, Ratcliffe is also the author of *The University of Virginia Football Vault: The History of the Cavaliers,* published in 2008. "Hootie" is now the editor of the popular JerryRatcliffe.com and the host of "The Jerry Ratcliffe Show," which airs on Saturdays at 9 a.m. on ESPN Charlottesville, 102.9 FM.

**Chris Graham** has covered UVA athletics since 1995. A 1994 graduate of the University of Virginia, he is also the co-author of *Mad About U: Four Decades of Basketball at University Hall,* a historical review of the famed former home of UVA basketball, published in 2006. Graham is the editor of AugustaFreePress.com, which launched in 2002, and a play-by-play broadcaster covering college baseball and college football for ESPN3 and ESPN+.

**Zach Pereles** covered the UVA basketball in 2019 for AugustaFreePress. com. A 2018 graduate of Northwestern University, he covered Northwestern's football and men's basketball teams from 2014-2018, a run that included him covering Northwestern's first ever NCAA Tournament berth in 2017. He has also written for Yahoo Sports and *Sports Illustrated,* and he recently completed a season as a digital media contributor for the Denver Broncos.

**Scott Ratcliffe** has covered UVA Athletics for more than a decade, and has been a correspondent for publications including the *Miami Herald, Philadelphia Daily News, Charlotte Observer, Newport News Daily Press, Raleigh News & Observer,* and *Tulsa World,* among others.

**Scott German** covers UVA Athletics for AugustaFreePress.com. Scott has been around the 'Hoos his whole life. As a reporter, he was on site for both of UVA basketball's Final Fours, in 1981 and 1984, and has covered UVA football in bowl games dating back to its first, the 1984 Peach Bowl.